The Persistent Activist

The Persistent Activist

How Peace Commitment Develops and Survives

James Downton Jr.
Paul Wehr

WestviewPress
A Division of HarperCollins*Publishers*

Copyright © 1997 by Westview Press, A Division of HarperCollins Publishers, Inc.

Published in 1997 in the United States of America by Westview Press, 5500 Central Avenue, Boulder, Colorado 80301-2877, and in the United Kingdom by Westview Press, 12 Hid's Copse Road, Cumnor Hill, Oxford OX2 9JJ

Library of Congress Cataloging-in-Publication Data
Downton, James V.
   The persistent activist : how peace commitment develops and
survives / James Downton, Jr. and Paul Wehr.
      p.   cm.
   Includes bibliographical references and index.
   ISBN 0-8133-8139-8 (hc.) — ISBN 0-8133-2999-X (pbk.)
   1. Peace.   2. Peace movements.   3. Pacifists.   I. Wehr, Paul
Ernest, 1937–   .   II. Title.
JX1953.3.D65   1997
327.1'72—dc21   96-53176
                                                                                          CIP

The paper used in this publication meets the requirements of the American National Standard for Permanence of Paper for Printed Library Materials Z39.48-1984.

10   9   8   7   6   5   4   3   2   1

*We dedicate this book to persistent peace and
social justice activists everywhere,
and especially to Anice Swift and Alex Mayer,
two activists who inspired others
through their exemplary peacemaking.*

CONTENTS

PREFACE

We are living at an unusual historical moment. A long period of cold war has given way to an uneasy peace of great political and economic uncertainty. The pattern of global politics looks quite different than it did a decade ago when the superpowers cast a threatening shadow of nuclear war over the political landscape. Though the structures of authority within and between nations are currently being rearranged, there is no assurance of peace and no reason to think that popular challenges to governments will subside in the future. Protest movements operating outside of normal politics will continue to be a major force for change as well as a constraint on those who govern.

We are also at a crucial point in our understanding of how social movements emerge, function, and decline. A cycle of protest lasting more than three decades has produced significant new analytical and experiential knowledge in the field of collective action. A large portion of citizens in the U.S. has now participated in protest politics and much scholarly work has been done to analyze and explain it. Unfortunately, social activists and collective action researchers have rarely worked together to produce knowledge that may be useful to movements. We feel that such collaboration is long overdue. We hope this book will encourage it.

We will be examining an aspect of collective action where an exchange between activist and researcher could be particularly useful. Maintaining participation in a social movement is of special interest to the leaders of movement organizations and to those who study them. Recruiting, then keeping, participants is particularly difficult for movements like the peace movement where the personal interests of peace workers are not consistently threatened and the public good they seek offers them little material reward. For instance, how does the peace movement maintain its vitality during inter-war periods when the public's interest in peace issues is low? How does it retain the commitment of its members and especially that small cadre of activists who keep it alive? How do those caretakers of the movement keep themselves going over the long term?

This study explores the movement experience of thirty Colorado peace activists, whose names we have changed to conceal their identities. What they teach us about movement participation should feed back into the peace movement to make it stronger and more effective. We have reviewed the research on movement participation, located our study within it, and developed a theory of sustained commitment as a possible contribution to collective action theory. Hoping to serve the activist and scholarly communities, we wanted to produce knowledge of both practical and theoretical value.

Activist and scholar alike may notice a common thread in the stories of these peace activists, which is that peace action evolves into an ethical career that is inseparable from personal identity and day-to-day life. Were we to discover that the commitments of participants in other movements develop and survive in ways similar to these peacemakers, we would be a step closer to a more general theory of persistent activism.

James Downton Jr.
Paul Wehr

ACKNOWLEDGMENTS

This study represents the contributions of many people. Our thirty respondents revealed to us invaluable knowledge of how and why people work for change through social movements. We are deeply grateful to them for sharing their lives with us. We also want to give special thanks to Mary Downton, who read the manuscript carefully and offered useful suggestions to improve it; to Ann Underwood, who transcribed the interviews; to Jan Buhrmann, who prepared the manuscript for publication; and to Guy Burgess for his help with the graphics. We also want to thank the University of Colorado's Council on Research and Creative Work and the Department of Sociology for providing funds for various stages of the project. Finally, we want to acknowledge each other, for the patience, good humor, and openness to change that emerged over the course of the project. Ours was an equal undertaking, which is why we are listed alphabetically as co-authors. It is no small achievement to emerge from such an enterprise with a stronger friendship and greater mutual respect.

J.D.
P.W.

1

PEACE ACTION

Peace activism can be a fleeting involvement on behalf of a single issue or a way of life. Activists know that it is a hard life of struggle and disappointments and a good life of meaning and community. Among those who become involved, only a hard core of people remain committed over the long term. They are the unwavering few who have made life careers out of nonviolent action and community organizing. This is a study of those persisters, people who have dedicated their lives to creating peace and social justice in the world. How they have maintained their commitment in the face of great odds and many disappointments is the interesting question we address.

Social movements are organized attempts by citizens to change the policies or structures of government when conventional means for attaining those ends have failed.[1] The contemporary peace movement in the U.S. developed over the decades of the 1960s, 1970s, and 1980s to pressure the government to end the Cold War with the Soviet Union, to change its policies in Vietnam and Latin America, and to alter its domestic policy so that the issues of poverty and political inequality could be more forcefully addressed. The broad goals of the peace movement include peace between nations and an end to violence, a more equitable distribution of economic and political resources within and between nations, and an appreciation for diversity of gender, race, and culture.

Inspired by the examples of Gandhi and Martin Luther King, Jr., the movement uses nonviolent methods to achieve those goals. It uses conventional means, such as lobbying legislators to force a change in policy or educating the public about peace issues to change public opinion. Often it applies unconventional nonviolent direct action such as civil disobedience to disrupt or shut down governmental operations. The movement attracts a variety of people, from radicals who want sweeping changes of the political system to people with more moderate views who are content to work within the system to change it. The movement includes large national organizations devoted to peace action, although its greatest strength lies in the energy of the many activists who work within small local groups to plan and carry out projects of peaceful change.

Our understanding of persistent peace activism may be enhanced through comparison with studies of other social movements, and our work may, in turn, contribute to a broader understanding of social activism. Therefore, we begin with a brief summary of the main currents of collective action theory, noting some of the existing research about participation in social movements. We then introduce our study and the peace activists who participated in it.

COLLECTIVE ACTION THEORIES

The development and maintenance of a peace activist's commitment needs to be placed in the context of what is known about collective action and participation in social movements. There are three sets of theories which attempt to explain why people are willing to challenge the structures of authority in society.

Social psychological theories emphasize the collective states of emotion and belief which sweep large numbers of people irrationally into collective action. Such people move outside of accepted, routinized patterns of behavior as a result of their psychological inclinations and the social disorganization of society around them, which cuts them loose from their normal integrated relationships. Social movement participants, in this view, are likely to be "floaters" or poorly integrated into society. Socially dislocated, they are susceptible to the irrational appeals of demagogues. Thus, social movements are thought to originate when new social problems, strains, and grievances develop in society, which give rise to social disorganization and the accompanying intensity of emotions which can cause people to behave in bizarre and destructive ways. Piven and Cloward refer to these views of collective behavior as "malintegration" theories, based on the idea that people who engage in social protest do so because they have not been properly integrated into the social order. As outsiders, they are more likely to think and behave irrationally as a consequence of their alienation.[2]

Rational choice theories offer an alternative explanation for the emergence of organized collective action. From this perspective, protest movements are viewed as rational, thoughtful responses to social grievances which are always present in society. Whether people act to change social structures in order to eliminate the conditions that offend them is determined by their assessment of the costs and benefits of social activism and their subsequent decision about whether to participate in it. One approach which emphasizes rational choice is resource mobilization theory. It focuses on social movement organizations and how they mobilize resources rationally for the attainment of specific goals. A related approach—political process theory—presents collective action as an interactive process where protesters and movements rationally confront the larger political system on its own conventional terms. For theorists who emphasize the rationality of activists, participation in social movements is not an aberrant process disconnected from normal politics, but an extension of it.

New Social Movements theory presents a third perspective of collective action. It holds that, while malintegrationist and rationalist explanations for why people participate in social movements are useful, they are inadequate. Theorists who take this third approach view post-World War II movements as qualitatively different from earlier ones. They see the conflicts around which those movements developed as new, emerging from structural changes and modernization processes which have steadily eroded the boundary between personal life and the public domain, between the individual and powerful organizations. Jurgen Habermas' concept of "life-world-invaded" is a cornerstone of this orientation.[3] From his point of view, by increasingly invading the private lives of individuals, the state and the corporation have unintentionally triggered their collective resistance and protest.

According to New Social Movements theorists, contemporary protesters are middle class in origin. This post-war breed of activists has responded to radically different conditions and new social strains. For example, the student movement, the women's liberation movement, and the environmental and peace movements introduced many new value-oriented issues and were largely populated by young, middle-class dissidents. They challenged the dominant moral tenets of society because, from their perspective, those principles led directly to inequality, war, and environmental abuse.

New Social Movements theorists would agree with the malin-tegrationists that the grievances which stimulate social discontent may arise from the conditions of a particular historical moment. Some periods of history will produce a greater variety of social protests and more intense activity than others, when the issues are less compelling. In this view, contemporary social movements would be different from earlier movements because of the unique issues they address. New Social Movement theorists would also argue that resource mobilization and political process theories are correct in assuming that activists are rational in analyzing social conditions, developing strategy, and mobilizing resources. They would see rationality in the way activists use existing political institutions to advance their causes at the same time that they recommend sweeping changes in them.

New Social Movements theory incorporates features from the social psychological and rationalist perspectives—the style of analyzing structural change, the essential dynamics of the mobilization process, and the emphasis on the historical context which leads to protest. It adds, however, a cultural dimension to our understanding of activism by suggesting that a social movement depends on the growth of a collective identity among its members, forged from their unique and common cultural experiences. Here, the importance of the personal dimension of activism is emphasized because it is the everyday life of the activist which produces, then reproduces, a movement's culture.

In the peace movement, the more committed participants may "live the movement" by creating a culture around the movement's goals and values. The scope of peace action may broaden, to where how one works and lives each day becomes as important as how much time is spent in movement activities. From this perspective, social movements develop as much from the emergence of a new culture in the members' everyday lives as in their interactions in carrying out projects and protests.

"Living the movement" would give new significance to what Melucci calls the "submerged life" of movement networks.[4] This activity has no formal connection to a movement yet reinforces commitment because it links a member's daily life to formal movement work. Examples would be activists spending time together hiking, developing a child care cooperative for their families, or starting a common garden. These daily activities reinforce community, which would tend to strengthen their commitment and movement work. This view reveals how resources are mobilized not only by the deliberate decisions of social movement organizations, but through networks of personal relationships and neighborhoods where individuals and small groups often invent movement projects and carry them out.

Together, the social psychological, rationalist, and New Social Movements perspectives provide a useful foundation for understanding how and why peace activists go outside of officially sanctioned ways of "doing" politics to challenge social structures and policies and how they maintain their commitment over time.[5] Here, we briefly introduce some of the general issues of collective action which bear on the participation and persistence of activists.

Why People Participate in Collective Action

Many people who benefit from social movements do not get directly involved in them. Some may not have the time to be active; others may hold back because of the risks involved, while still others may be offended by some aspect of a movement's ideology or method of protest. But the largest group of nonparticipants are those known as "free riders" in collective action research. They refrain from joining because they quite rationally anticipate reaping the rewards won by a movement without any personal effort or risk.[6] Yet, many people do participate in collective action for various reasons, partly to serve the public good but also because of the "selective incentives" a movement provides. These are the personal rewards that activism offers the activist: The opportunity to openly express deeply-held beliefs and values, a sense of solidarity and connection with others of a similar ideological persuasion, membership in an organization working for a change which seems desirable, even the development of useful organizing skills.

Fear and hope can also motivate people to take part in collective action. For instance, the belligerent rhetoric and militant superpower policies of the early years of Ronald Reagan's presidency heightened people's fear of nuclear war to the point where they felt compelled to work to end the arms race. Hope of success also impelled people into peace action. The early success of local FREEZE movements in mobilizing public opinion against the nuclear threat convinced some that they might be able to move policy-makers toward arms reductions.[7] However, failure of that change to materialize also discouraged many, leading to the surge-and-slump dynamic that Lofland describes in detail.[8]

People are also drawn into social movements through the effective recruitment efforts of movement organizations. Those organizations range from large national organizations with professional staffs which manage broad campaigns, to small local groups that plan and carry out actions independent of the national movement.

Success in recruitment is often determined by factors beyond a movement's control, such as the Three Mile Island and Chernobyl accidents that greatly stimulated anti-nuclear activism. Especially important is a movement organization's ability to keep the activist engaged with a meaningful conceptual framework for analyzing conditions it seeks to alter and a mechanism for changing them. In fact, leaders of an organization may have to alter its framework over time to adapt to changing conditions and opportunities. They must also present their particular way of framing problems and solutions to specific groups outside of the movement to recruit new members.[9]

Why Some Activists Persist

While collective action researchers have learned much about how members are recruited during movement mobilization, little is known about what keeps some active over the long term. To understand such persistence, three types of information about long-term peace activism are needed: The national and global contexts within which it takes place; the local settings in which the persisters' lives and movement work are carried out; and the personal attributes and life experiences which set them on a course which eventually leads to an activist career.

National and Global Contexts. It is important to consider the impact of the larger political and economic situation on the development of social movements and how they mobilize and retain members. These "macromobilization contexts" can heavily influence the opportunities for activism and the expansion of social movements. In the case of peace action, wars can mobilize thousands of people in a short time, expanding the rolls of existing peace groups or producing new ones as individuals seek an outlet for their ideas, anger, and fears. Also, economic and political opportunities at the national level can influence local activism. For example, a growing economy in the 1980s increased foundation grants for local movement organizations, discretionary time and income for its members, and opportunities for movement entrepreneurship in towns and cities across the country. This support would have encouraged the long-term commitment of peace activists.

Political opportunities for nonviolent action also improved during the 1980s, for the government's willingness to tolerate nonviolent protest had been increasing steadily, as it learned to respond to demonstrations without using police violence. In fact, peace activists in the 1980s were seen by many citizens and public officials as valuable critics of national policy. The movement's imaginative use of nonviolent action established a degree of public credibility for it, which peace movement leaders learned to exploit as political opportunity shifted between local and national levels.[10] The development of new "structures of political opportunity" would be likely to increase long-term activism.[11]

Local Action Contexts. While conditions in the world, nation and region may encourage peace action, they are not sufficient to produce a long-term commitment among activists. Persistence develops in the local settings where activists do their movement work: Peace groups, churches, workplaces, friendship networks, schools, food cooperatives, and parenting groups. These are the local settings for recruitment and on-going participation in social movements, what McAdam and others call "micromobilization contexts."[12] Through these local activities, collective identity develops, a sense of community flourishes, the altruism so essential for deepening commitment is reinforced, and movement goals and commitment are secured by the development of close personal ties between activists.

Social movement organizations also provide resources which help activists persist, such as a subsistence income as a movement worker, the security and well-being derived from community membership, and psychological support during difficult times. An activist may be part of a permanent cadre who staff what Morris calls "caretaker" organizations,[13] groups such as the American Friends Service Committee (AFSC) which provide support and encouragement to the peace movement during its lean years.

Personal Attributes and Life Experiences. How does personal history contribute to a career in peace action? To understand what keeps activists involved over the long term, it is important to know about their personal attributes and life experiences, the character of their beliefs, how they came to the movement, and their life styles, including how they earn a living. Benchmark events along a person's life course are important information. Were there personal experiences with injustice or violence which led to their indictment of mainstream institutions? Were there movement leaders or writers who influenced their thinking?

Collective action research is just beginning to identify the personal attributes that contribute to long-term activism. McAdam's study of civil rights activists describes how people come to and stay in movement work, free from economic and other constraints, attitudinally affiliated with movement goals, and located within networks of political activism.[14] Schwartz discusses the psychological process by which a sympathizer becomes an activist through awareness of the consequences action might have and subsequent development of a sense of personal responsibility to act.[15]

The duration and depth of one's experience with social activism may also help explain how commitment forms and is kept alive. For example, long-term members of a movement may be so thoroughly socialized into the activist role that they can no longer separate themselves from it. Lofland's research suggests that when the activist role has been fully embraced, activism becomes a way of life and of thinking, which merge in a new conception of self.[16] This type of transformative experience may also occur through dramatic marking experiences, as it did with civil rights activists in the Freedom Summer project.[17]

These general issues about social movement participation informed our thinking as we conceived our study and developed our interview questions. Our goal was to develop a theory of sustained commitment from the stories of peace activists that, while focused on the peace movement, would be applicable to other social movements as well. What we learn from these activists may help us understand the continuity of activist commitments generally. It may, as well, increase in a modest way the effectiveness of the peace movement and other social movements seeking to improve the quality of human life.

THE STUDY

This work draws upon collective action theory and on our earlier paper, "Peace Movements: The Role of Commitment and Community in Sustaining Member Participation."[18] There, we explore commitment as a process of bonding to various sectors of the peace movement: Leadership, ideology, organizations, rituals, and friendship groups. We argue that an individual may initially become involved in the peace movement as a result of attraction to one or more of these sectors. For example, a person may like the way the movement is organized or feel its ideology is compelling. These initial points of attraction may expand to include the leaders of the group, community rituals, and friendship networks. It is important to understand the intensity of commitment in any one of these areas, but also the extent of commitment, or how much loyalty a person feels across all five areas. Kendrick's research also shows the significance of these ties in the recruitment and retention of activists.[19]

While our earlier work on bonding was a useful theoretical beginning, this study expands our concerns to a wider range of influences which affect the development and persistence of a peace career. By studying the experiences of a group of Colorado peace activists, we hoped to identify factors besides bonding which contribute to the persistence of activism. We wanted to learn what influences determined who would persist, who would shift to other movements, and who would drop out of activism completely.

While all three of these groups are included in this study, our primary concern was to learn what causes activists to stay with the peace movement over the long term. There is little research on persistent activists, yet their role in collective action is central because they constitute the hard core of organizers who keep social movements alive. What is the process by which commitment to peace activism develops for these people and how is it preserved over their activist careers?

Our interviews were conducted in 1992 and 1993 during a period of diminished peace activism. The Cold War had ended with the disintegration of the Soviet Union, so the threat of nuclear war was significantly reduced; the Contra War in Nicaragua had stopped; nuclear testing in Nevada had ceased; the Persian Gulf War in 1991 had ended quickly; and a decision had been made by the federal government to close the Rocky Flats nuclear weapons plant in Colorado, the site of many peace demonstrations over the years. So, our activists were interviewed at a time of pause, which affected the nature of their responses to our questions.

Data Gathering

Potential participants in the study were identified by consulting with four well-established peace movement organizations from two communities. We drew half of our respondents from a small city with a major university and half from a large urban center. Twenty activists were chosen who had remained committed to peace action for more than five years and were still active in the movement. For comparison, we also interviewed ten activists who had left peace action after several years' involvement, four for other movements and six who had withdrawn from activism entirely. Gender seemed like it might be a relevant factor, so our respondents were selected to achieve a fairly even gender distribution.

We gathered our data with a semi-structured interview guide (see Appendix). Interviews with the participants occurred over a period of several months, each lasting from one to two hours. Interviews were recorded and transcribed. Content was coded for relevant themes and recurring concepts, then organized using the Ethnograph, a qualitative data-organizing computer program.[20]

Our study has clear limitations. It is exploratory, so it is limited in scope. We worked with a small number of activists and organizations within a single movement and at a time of diminished peace activism. While our respondents were selected from two quite different communities, they were from a single metropolitan area. We are not, therefore, claiming that our findings can be generalized beyond the groups studied. We hope, nevertheless, that this book will advance an underdeveloped line of collective action research and theory—persistent activism— that others might find useful.

The Participants

Our respondents are an interesting group of people from different parts of the U.S., from different social classes, and with diverse types of peace work to their credit. Eighteen of them are female and twelve are male. While they range in age from 24 to 86, a preponderance of them are in their forties (43%), fifties (13%), and sixties (20%). Judging from how and when most of them came to peace action, we can identify a cohort coming of political age during the 1965-75 period of U.S. history when there was a major surge of social protest.

Our participants are highly educated, with twenty (66%) having earned advanced university degrees. But they are not well paid for that academic investment. Their income distribution tends toward the low end of the scale. Often, they were unable to calculate their incomes precisely, erratic and scattered as the latter appeared to be. In addition, those incomes higher on the scale tended to be joint incomes. These modest incomes, set against high educational achievement, reflected the conscious decision of many to live a simple material life as a central feature of their peace careers.

The occupational profile of these activists is diverse. It includes mixed countercultural and conventional worlds of work, low paying jobs within peace movement organizations, and regular nine-to-five employment. Many worked conventional jobs only part-time so they were free to pursue peace action. Some earned a meager income from canvassing neighborhoods for peace causes, leading nonviolence trainings, organizing protests, and providing mediation services. What Anthony Oberschall calls the "free professions" are clearly represented among our participants: Lawyers, university faculty, and writers.[21] The helping professions are also well represented: Social worker, physician, health worker, and medical secretary. Even the IBM systems engineer and the university administrator are there. Alongside these professionals are the tea taster, the migrant labor coordinator, and the professional herbalist.

Our activists' average length of participation in peace action is 20 years. Together they represent a total of 524 years in the movement. Octogenarian Martha began her activist career with Jane Addams' Hull House in Chicago in the 1920s and came to the peace movement in the early 1950s.

While our sample includes a diverse range of people, a common thread binds two-thirds of them. They are peace action persisters, who are unable to imagine their lives without peace work.

The Communities

Our participants were drawn in equal numbers from Denver and Boulder. Denver is a city of half a million people with an equal number living in its suburbs. It is a commercial and financial center and a transportation hub for the Rocky Mountain west. Thirty miles to the northwest lies Boulder, a city of 100,000 people centered around the University of Colorado. A large number of computer and biotechnology firms are located there.

Two conditions in particular encouraged the development of a large peace-attentive community in Colorado. First, the state has been host to many military installations and several weapons corporations. Three in particular—the Rocky Flats nuclear weapons plant, the NORAD air defense center, and the Martin Marietta missile program—contributed heavily to the U.S. nuclear war fighting capability in the 1980s. Second, environmental activism is well developed in Colorado. The environmental and peace movements often find common cause, as they did in the campaign to shut down Rocky Flats.

The Organizations

While our activists were members of about 30 peace movement organizations, their peace action was largely concentrated in the four organizations through which we contacted them. The American Friends Service Committee (AFSC) Colorado Regional Program is a Quaker service organization, part of the national AFSC. Colorado branches of Peace Action (formerly SANE FREEZE) and the Women's International League for Peace and Freedom (WILPF) are parts of national organizations with substantial memberships. The Rocky Mountain Peace Center in

Boulder is a local organization linked with other peace and social justice centers in the West.

THE THREE ACTIVIST GROUPS

Persisters. As we defined them, "persisters" had to have been continuously active in peace work for at least five years, although, in fact, most had been active for much longer periods of time. They had to be directly involved in the peace movement by assuming an active role in a peace group, which might include organizing projects, participating in actions, and educating the public about peace issues. Peace-making efforts in other areas of life, such as being a mediator, did not qualify as peace activism by our definition, unless the person was also active in a peace movement organization.

As later chapters will reveal, the commitment of persisters develops in ways similar to those who do not persist, but it endures because it becomes an integral part of their identities and ways of living. While persisters build peace action carefully into their lives, "shifters" and "dropouts" seem less inclined to do so.

Shifters. The shifters are activists who left peace action for another social cause. They may perceive their new work as peace action, especially if they are working on the issue of violence. However, as just noted, to be identified as a persister in this study, the individual had to continue to be involved in the peace movement. Given their strong sense of responsibility to solve social problems, shifters are likely to be career activists, but outside of the peace movement.

Dropouts. The dropouts are those who left activism altogether. Why they left is one of the important questions we address in this study. The dropout label should be regarded with caution, however, for some may leave the peace movement temporarily, returning when a new war develops or a personal problem, which drew them out of activism, has been resolved.

DEVELOPING A PEACE CAREER

Social activism is similar to a normal career in many ways. A person must have the aptitude for the job, the career evolves in definite stages, and it persists because many personal and social factors maintain it. In the following chapters, the peace careers of persisters will be examined in detail as part of this larger commitment-building process. We will discover how they became ethically prepared for peace action, how they became involved in the movement, how their peace activist identity emerged to reinforce their commitment, how they grew personally from their activism, and how they learned to deal with disappointments and burnout so their peace careers could survive. One thing common to most persisters was their inability to visualize their lives without peace action. Many felt that working for peace and social change was what they were meant to do. Whether their motivation was humanistic, religious or a mix of the two, they were activists because they had to be for their own peace of mind. As David, a persister, said: "The commitment itself is very important, but satisfaction is pretty important too, knowing that one is doing what one almost has to do, or feels one can't get along without doing."

NOTES

1. We use the term "social movement" interchangeably with "protest movement," emphasizing that "protest" is a term used broadly to include a range of activities, from unconventional actions that lead to police intervention and arrest to more conventional tactics such as lobbying for important legislation. A "social activist" is someone who becomes involved in a social movement in order to change the policies or structures of government through these various forms of collective action. A "peace activist" is a social activist who engages in collective action to achieve the goals of peace and social justice.

2. Frances Fox Piven and Richard Cloward, "Normalizing Collective Protest," in Aldon Morris and Carol Mueller, eds., *Frontiers of Modern Social Movement Theory*. (New Haven: Yale University Press, 1992), pp. 301-325.

3. Habermas uses Husserl's life-world concept to illustrate how state interventions in formerly private areas of life stimulated collective action in response. See Jurgen Habermas, *Toward a Rational Society*. (Boston: Beacon Press, 1970).

4. Alberto Melucci, "The Process of Collective Identity." A paper presented at the Workshop on Culture and Social Movements, University of California, San Diego (June, 1992), p. 15.

5. We are particularly indebted in this section to a fine review of collective action research in Doug McAdam, John McCarthy and Mayer Zald, "Social Movements," in Neil Smelser, ed., *Handbook of Sociology.* (Beverly Hills, CA: Sage Publications, 1988), pp. 695-737.

6. The free rider concept is developed in Mancur Olson, *The Logic of Collective Action: Public Goods and the Theory of Groups.* (Cambridge, MA: Harvard University Press, 1965).

7. Byron Miller, "Political Empowerment, Local-central State Relations, and Geographically Shifting Political Opportunity Structures," *Political Geography,* 13 (1994), pp. 393-406.

8. John Lofland, "The Soar and Slump of Polite Protest: Interactive Spirals and the Eighties Peace Surge," *Peace and Change,* 17 (1992), pp. 34-59.

9. For a discussion of the framing process, see David Snow, E. Burke Rochford, Jr. Steven Worden, and Robert Benford, "Frame Alignment Processes, Micromobilization and Movement Participation," *American Sociological Review,* 51 (1986), pp. 464-481.

10. Miller, *op. cit.*

11. The concept of opportunity structure is used by Tarrow and others to analyze points of public access to policymaking, for example, changes in government presenting new openings for political influence through collective action. We extend the concept here to describe opportunities for such action at the level of the individual activist. Sidney Tarrow, "Struggle, Politics and Reform: Collective Action, Social Movements and Cycles of Protest," Western Societies Program Paper No. 21. (Ithaca, NY: Cornell University Press, 1989).

12. Doug McAdam, "Micromobilization Contexts and Recruitment to Activism," in Bert Klandermans, Hanspeter Kriesi and Sidney Tarrow, eds., *International Social Movement Research: Volume 1.* (Greenwich, CT: JAI Press, 1988), pp. 125-154.

13. Aldon Morris, *Origins of the Civil Rights Movement.* (New York: The Free Press, 1984).

14. Doug McAdam, *Freedom Summer: The Idealists Revisited,* Chapter 2. (New York: Oxford University Press, 1988).

15. See S. H. Schwartz, "Words, Deeds and the Perception of Consequences and Responsibility in Action Situations," *Journal of Personality and Social Psychology,* 10 (1968), pp. 232-242; Joseph Hopper and Joyce McCarl Nielsen, "Recycling as Altruistic Behavior," *Environment and Behavior,* 23 (1991), pp. 195-220; G. Marwell, "Altruism and the Problem of Collective Action," in V. Derlega and J. Grzelak, eds., *Cooperation and Helping Behavior.* (New York: Academic Press, 1982), pp. 13-37.

16. John Lofland, *Doomsday Cult*. (Englewood Cliffs, NJ: Prentice-Hall, 1966).

17. Doug McAdam, "The Biographical Consequences of Activism," *American Sociological Review*, 54 (1989), p. 751.

18. James V. Downton, Jr. and Paul E. Wehr, "Peace Movements: The Role of Commitment and Community in Sustaining Member Participation," in Metta Spencer, ed., *Research in Social Movements, Conflicts, and Change*, Vol. 13, (Greenwich, CT: JAI Press, 1991), pp. 113-134.

19. See his interactive model of participation in J. Richard Kendrick, Jr., "Meaning and Participation: Perspectives of Peace Movement Participants," in Spencer, *op. cit.*, pp. 91-111.

20. John V. Seidel, Rolf Kjolseth and Elaine Seymour, *The Ethnograph*, (Qualis Research Associates). John Seidel can be reached by writing to him at P.O. Box 2070, Amherst, MA, 01004, or through EMAIL: Seidel @QualisResearch.com. One can also see a demonstration of the Ethnograph and get information about ordering the software on his website: http://www. QualisResearch.com.

21. Anthony Oberschall, *Social Conflict and Social Movements*. (Englewood Cliffs, NJ: Prentice-Hall, 1973), p. 152.

2

BELIEFS AND PEACE ACTION

Peace activism is an ethical career which develops over time. It is ethical because it is guided by moral principles, such as loving your neighbor, resolving conflicts without violence, and creating communities based on mutual respect, equality, cooperation, and social justice. Like other careers, a peace career has a beginning, develops a unique form, and thrives because many personal and social factors emerge to support it. On the personal level, certain beliefs need to develop over an individual's lifetime which establish the moral basis for peace action. Developing those beliefs is an essential step for continuing as a peace activist, even in the face of serious setbacks and discouraging national and international news. How those beliefs form is the focus of this chapter.

THE CREATION OF PEACE-ORIENTED BELIEFS

Perhaps no concept is more important for understanding commitment and its continuity than belief. Beliefs are ideas we are socialized to think are true and it is their truth-laden meaning which gives them the power to shape our perception of social reality and to affect our behavior. Beliefs are essentially of two types: Those about what is (facts) and those about what should be (morality).

Beliefs provide us with a mental frame of reference so we can more easily interpret and give meaning to what we see, what we feel, and what we do. In essence, beliefs are thought patterns which govern the way we understand ourselves, others and the institutions of society.

Perhaps the most important fact of human functioning is that human beings have the capacity to think and what a person thinks has the power to shape personal reality. 'As a man thinks, so it shall be' is a very profound statement of fact because thought is the link between a human being and the reality in which that human being lives.[1]

Beliefs arise during the early stages of socialization and, to borrow from Berger and Luckman,[2] become the foundation of our social constructions of reality. Beliefs are created by groups in order to establish an orientation to other groups in the social world, to develop goals and courses of action, to respond to threat, to carry on the life of community, and to find a place in the cosmos. In part, beliefs make up the essential ideological architecture of groups as they cooperate and struggle with one another.

While beliefs are "made up" gradually over time, those who are socialized to adopt them remain in ignorance of their essentially fictional nature. They live within those beliefs as if they were an objective depiction of what they are seeing, hearing, and understanding. Those beliefs, as patterns of thought which establish the "truth" to be passed on from one generation to another, are fundamental for understanding what draws people into peace careers and why they stay there.

The personal accounts of our activists reveal that prolonged peace activism is enhanced when beliefs exist which establish:

- ❖ an ethical ground for peace action, including the beliefs (values) that it's "good" to love your neighbor and to use nonviolent means for resolving conflicts, and that social justice for all classes, races, and genders is the morally correct condition;
- ❖ a fair degree of separation from conventional society, expressed as opposition to governmental and social arrangements which need thorough transformation;
- ❖ the perception that political activism is necessary to solve pressing problems such as social injustice or war;
- ❖ a strong sense of personal responsibility to work for peace and to change society;
- ❖ a sense of urgency for peace and social justice work as compared to other pressing social issues, such as overpopulation, energy depletion, and environmental decline;

❖ an ethical orientation and activist identity which create a sense of mission and give meaning to life;

❖ the perception that the peace movement is having a positive impact on local, national, and international policy;

❖ a sense of assurance that, through gradual changes, a transformation of society toward peace will occur over time.

Persisters acquired these beliefs over the course of their peace careers, but several were embraced in their youth and early adulthood. How did those beliefs develop and how did they shape the persisters' sense of social reality and their emotions? How did they influence what they chose to do? And how did those choices, taken together, become commitments? In this chapter, we explore the socialization influences that helped shape the beliefs which set persisters on a course toward peace action.

SOCIALIZATION INFLUENCES

A peace and social justice career does not evolve the same way for each person; on the contrary, what is interesting is the unique configuration of each career as different socialization influences come to bear on the individual.

Learning to Help Others and Take Action

Several persisters had childhood experiences in the family, church and school which taught them the values of loving and helping others. This altruism was often reinforced by role models, sometimes a parent, teacher, or minister, who exemplified a life dedicated to caring.

The Family. Michael, a 60 year old persister, was raised by religious parents who taught him to take responsibility for helping others. This belief led him into a religious life and eventually he graduated from seminary. The belief was also a source of disillusionment over society's inability to realize its loftier principles. "I had been raised with the idea that human beings should care for each other. You should love yourself and your neighbor. I took that seriously. When I discovered the extent to which that wasn't happening, I was unhappy."

Michael was more than unhappy; he was angry. Such anger, not uncommon among persisters, arose from the gap between their deeply held ethical values and the way they saw society operating. The belief that "human beings should care for each other" established a frame of reference for evaluating society. Holding this belief, they discovered a disturbing gap between the ideal and reality, a discontinuity which served to stir emotions and motivate action.

Without an ethic of action, the gap between ideals and reality could lead to cynicism. Cynics are idealists who, lacking a sufficiently strong sense of responsibility to take action, remain passive but highly critical. Unlike cynics, persisters came to believe that it was their duty to help others and that collective action was an effective course for solving social problems. This combination of beliefs launched them into social criticism and eventually forced them to do something about the conditions they deplored.

Sometimes the family experiences of persisters combined training in the ethics of helping others with exposure to a parent who was politically active. Ruth, a 66 year old persister, recalled how her mother, who was a social worker during the Great Depression, would come home at night "utterly crushed" by the plight of the poor people she worked with. Her mother joined the social workers union and "then a lot of people would visit our home and talk about politics." It was through these experiences and the influence of her mother that Ruth developed a concern for others. Exposed to human suffering and political conversation in this way as a child, she formed her initial beliefs about peace and social justice.

Other persisters were introduced by their parents to a more direct type of political education. Matt was raised in "a fairly volatile Irish Catholic family" where, as the youngest, he "was always trying to make deals with the adversaries" in order to resolve conflicts. His father held strong political beliefs, which he taught to his children. He had grown up in Ireland in a revolutionary time and he possessed a global political perspective. Matt remembered him giving his family "a broader picture of how the world worked, how imperialism worked and how people were oppressed."

Learning to be responsible for helping the disadvantaged and oppressed was a central feature of persister careers. Michael, Ruth, and Matt learned this from their parents. So did Diane, a 45 year old persister from a working class family. She was part of a "big, poor family," where her parents taught her to be grateful for being alive and to feel a sense of responsibility for helping others. "It's not everybody that's raised by two parents who care about each other and care about their kids and try to instill in them some good values."

Although Diane was raised to believe that she was responsible for others, this was not translated into peace action until other conditions were present. Later, she turned to peace action as a result of her experiences as a teacher and the influence of Martin Luther King, Jr., the Catholic Worker movement, and leading Catholic pacifists such as Dorothy Day, Daniel Berrigan, and Thomas Merton. This points up the fact that, while parents may teach their children "good values," that is only a foundation. Other influences must develop to turn that ethical potential for social action into reality.

Religion. The church was another place where activists learned to "love your neighbor," although it sometimes failed to live up to its own values. Sally, a 42 year old persister, recalled: "The religious tradition that I come from, Catholicism, teaches concern about helping others, although I sometimes thought the practice didn't always live up to the ideal. But at least I got that kind of concern about taking care of your brothers and sisters."

During Diane's college years, many changes were made within the Catholic Church as a consequence of Vatican II. Her parish was fairly progressive, so she was exposed to the dramatic changes taking place in Latin America where priests and lay clergy were joining with the poor to create a new kind of political leverage. Their "Liberation Theology," a revolutionary interpretation of the Gospel, was an invitation for Catholics who sought permission and inspiration to carry out social justice reforms.

> We talked about work for social justice and peace as a constitutive element of the Gospel. The friends of God are the poor and those who are friends of the poor. So it seems to me that's kind of a big part of why I would want to be involved in working for social justice and peace. It doesn't seem right that some people have everything and some have nothing, and I'd like to see a world where that is less the case.

For persisters like Diane, whose commitment to peace and

social justice grew out of religious faith, the radical reinterpreta-
tion of the Gospel was a dramatic development. It offered a
compelling religious justification for helping others through
political action and protest. It put God on the side of the
reformers rather than with the defenders of the church hierarchy
and the status quo. With this justification in hand, Catholics
could move more easily from the belief in helping others into
direct social action.

There were other religious influences as well. A 42 year old
career activist, Brian believed in helping others partly out of the
"strong ethical tradition in Judaism" which taught him to take
"responsibility for one's fellow man." Born in 1945, he grew up
hearing much about the Holocaust and the terrible things that
happened to his people. "As I got older," he recalled, "I felt I had
a special obligation to do what I could to change things so that
other people would not suffer in that way."

The religious influence on persisters was not uniformly
strong, but, where it existed, it had a major impact on the
development of their beliefs, including the responsibility to empathize with the oppressed, and then to do something to improve
their condition.

Education. Education played a key role in teaching persisters
to be more critical of society, the status quo, and the authorities
who work to preserve it. Their college experience was especially
important. It informed them about global issues and convinced
them to become involved in purposive social change taking place
at home and abroad. Criticism of the existing order is something
all persisters developed, although in varying degrees.

All of our respondents were college graduates, many with
advanced degrees. They were products of an educational system
which permitted and often encouraged critical thinking and a
commitment to social change. During the high pressure years of
movement activity during the 1960s and 1970s, they were taught
by some of their teachers to think critically, to take responsibility, and to act. Jonathan, a 70 year old persister who went to
college later in his life, learned this: "I feel that we live in a social
system that is very unjust and corrupt and that there comes a
time when you just have to stand up and be counted."

Unlike Ruth, Matt, and Diane, Jonathan was raised in a conservative family, where social criticism was seldom heard and

awareness of social issues was limited. He was introduced to such issues in high school. His eyes were opened to poverty and racism, which led him to the view that political arrangements in the world "didn't seem right and were disastrous for many subjected people." He began then to realize that something had to be done to bring about peace, but also more economic justice for the poor and better relationships between people.

Much later in college, Jonathan was exposed to teachers and books which made him question the existing social order more critically, especially in relation to the Vietnam War.

> I was radicalized in college. It became obvious that we were in Vietnam just to protect our interests at the expense of the native people who were already fighting for self-determination, and that we were using high-level technology to kill millions of people without any real justification.

Jonathan's educational experiences and the anti-war climate of the time shaped his social awareness, including his belief that "we live in a culture which seems worse than it was back in the '60s, where the dominant political and economic forces gobble everything up and the media corrupts everything."

In one form or another, this critical attitude was held by all our activists, although its intensity varied. This posture of social criticism had two important effects on their commitment: First, it put them at odds with the existing social order, creating the emotional intensity to seek to change it; second, the resulting sense of estrangement from national policies became an important feature of the peace culture, as people with similar critiques came together around their common views and ideals.

Many teachers, as well as students, received their political education during the Vietnam War, as people were called upon to take a moral stand. Diane was drawn into peace activism as a result of that pressure. During the war she was teaching a high school social problems course where she could not avoid discussing the war. This drew her into the debate, a moral nerve was touched, and she soon found herself on an anti-war committee. The war, by the sheer magnitude of its social impact, pulled her into peace action.

"Question Authority" was a popular slogan of the radical counterculture during the 1960s. Many persisters embraced it as a guide for their lives. If their parents or church failed to instill this notion, their education succeeded. At the heart of their ethical training was a commitment to caring for others, but, partly as a result of the failure of conventional politics to solve the social problems of the day, they became more willing to embrace nonviolence as a tactic for creating social change.

There were different nonviolent approaches available for them in the diverse activities of the peace movement. While persisters embraced similar goals, they were able to choose the means of goal attainment which fit their life situations, the level of risk they were willing to undertake, and their own ethical standards. Some engaged in confrontational actions and were arrested; others served in groups where peace education was the primary activity. Such educational enclaves were pockets of activism where nonviolence was still the operating principle, but where the confrontational methods of protest were avoided, perhaps because of the risk involved or because of ethical opposition to more forceful tactics.

Social Movements. The counterculture, civil rights, the Vietnam War, the student revolt, the environmental movement and feminism: It was hard to remain untouched by at least one of these currents of social change during the 1960s and 1970s. We have already seen the effect of the Vietnam War on some of our activists; but there were also other influences, most notably the civil rights movement. It had an important effect on Michael's political awareness. He had read Martin Luther King, Jr.'s "Letter from the Birmingham Jail" and had been "profoundly influenced" by it. Although not directly involved in civil rights protests, he began to speak out in support of them at the theological seminary where he was teaching. This got him "into a lot of trouble."

Through the 1960s, every movement that came along seemed to touch Michael. All were, in his eyes, about human survival. Given the global and national crises he was witnessing, he became aware that he had to do something. In this frame of mind, he was ready for a shift toward peace action.

In the summer of 1970, he came across Joan Bondurant's *Conquest of Violence* and began reading it. He recognized "that Gandhi had evolved a way of being political where truth is something we seek not something we possess. The idea that Gandhi's whole approach to nonviolence was the quest for truth just went to my core and immediately made enormous sense."

This was the turning point in the formation of Michael's peace career. Influenced by Gandhi's thought and example, he began to teach a course about nonviolence with an Indian scholar. This drew him into a serious study of the subject, which affected his religious outlook and eventually led him to abandon organized religion.

The various movements underway during that time pointed out blatant social injustice. They challenged people to assess their ethical positions and to take a stand. Brian remembered the powerful impact the civil rights movement had on him, when he saw on television what was happening in the segregated South. He became aware that the society he had learned about in school, one protecting freedom, democracy, and civil rights, was a sham. "The contrast between those ideals and the images of Bull Connor and the police dogs attacking people who were simply trying to put those ideals into practice—I think that's what motivated me to become involved in activism initially."

More Complete Stories

Several accounts of individual persisters are presented more fully here, in order to show how the social forces just described operate in unique ways to form a peace commitment.

Martha. An 85 year old persister, Martha was not well-informed about world affairs as a child. In fact, she lived a sheltered life in a conservative family, whose members applauded the young men volunteering for World War I and where her father's reactionary politics were hardly hidden from her.

> My father belonged to the Ku Klux Klan. He and other Klan members were burning crosses in black neighborhoods. Some of them didn't want Catholics around either. But my father had his costume in the bottom drawer of his chest and when I was 8 or 9 years old I found out he was in the Ku Klux Klan, and I wanted to wear it for Halloween, but he wouldn't let me.

Unlike her father, Martha's mother was "very broad-minded" and felt sympathy toward the poor, which strongly influenced Martha's ethical outlook. She recalled summer vacations in the Ozarks at the family cabin. As it was located near a railroad track, "hobos" making their way along the tracks often came to the back door for a handout. It was known to be a place where they would be received with kindness, for hobos had put their marks on the back gate to tell others passing by that "this is a good place to stop for a meal." Her mother never turned a hobo away and Martha always enjoyed having these downwardly mobile travelers show up at the back door. She learned from her mother's example that people "deserve to have a meal" and not to "be afraid of people just because they're in rags." Her mother's belief that "you should treat others as you want to be treated" was passed along to Martha and it became the ethical basis for her later activist career.

Given this mixed background of a politically reactionary father and a socially conscious mother, what were the later influences which turned Martha toward peace and social justice? One influence was the man she married. He had been a conscientious objector in World War I and he became a founding member of the American Civil Liberties Union.

A more important influence was her role as a teacher. In the 1950s, she was warned by her school board not to talk about the United Nations in her classes. This only served to awaken Martha's resistance. She began to think, "there must be a way around that. If the stodgy old school board doesn't want me to do it, it must be the way to go." This conflict was a test for Martha, who was forced to ask: "What am I for? Where do I stand? What am I going to work for?" That soul searching led her not only to discuss the United Nations with her students but to create the Model United Nations program. This conflict with "the stodgy old school board" was the turning point where Martha began her peace career.

June. A 54 year old persister, June turned to activism later in life. She grew up in a small midwestern community in a family which did not emphasize activism. In college, she could not remember being particularly aware of much beyond her day-to-day life. Even as a teacher in the Denver public schools, she was not socially aware. Things began to change when she joined the League of Women Voters, where she became "convinced that nuclear power was the wrong way to go, because of the long term ramifications of what it was. It was just wrong."

About that time, she learned about Cesar Chavez and the on-going grape boycott through her church. She began to read about the boycott and became concerned about the issues it was raising. She decided to talk to the manager of her local grocery about the store's policy, whether it would continue, and what the store might be doing to look into the issue. The manager's response was a hostile one, which surprised her because she had not questioned in an aggressive way. "I decided to quit shopping there. There was something about that situation that made me think that this work might be something important to do."

This was a turning point. When June became better informed about the grape boycott she began to speak to others about the issues and to persuade them to join it. This reinforced her emerging social activism, which eventually led her to participate in the Colorado Coalition, a group of prominent citizens who were working to eliminate nuclear weapons.

Jack. Unlike most of our persisters, Jack, a 68 year old career activist, was immersed in peace issues from childhood. His father was a pacifist and a Norman Thomas socialist, who took an active role in educating his children about political issues. Jack remembered his father reading radical articles at every evening meal, about disenfranchised minorities, migrant workers, and sharecroppers living in miserable conditions. His father emphasized the importance of taking personal responsibility for solving those problems and working to "bring about a peaceful society and to eliminate some of the roots of hunger and war."

Jack was also "raised in a strong church atmosphere." The Methodist church his family attended was oriented to peace issues during the 1930s when he was growing up. The youth group in his church "didn't veer away from pacifism; in fact, they encouraged it." He went to church youth camps each summer, where working for peace became a strong part of the program. "At the end of those retreats, you'd write yourself a commitment about how you would believe in peace and work for peace. Then the following year, you'd get a card from the church to see how you were doing with your commitment." By his early teens, he had already developed the beliefs which are essential for prolonged peace action.

Don. A 60 year old persister, Don had the strong religious training of Jack, but not the activist influence, so his peace career developed differently and much later in life. He grew up in a devoutly Catholic family and decided at age 20 to become a Jesuit priest. He spent 13 years in training, which included three years as a teacher, since the Jesuits are primarily a teaching order. During that time, he was politically uninformed and inactive. The seminary neither encouraged nor supported political work and he had little contact with the media because of the reclusive nature of his training. "I think I got a very strong moral and ethical sense from my whole Catholic background and Jesuit training," he noted. "But no one really helped me to see what that meant as far as the social order was concerned."

Don's case is interesting because it demonstrates how having an ethical foundation does not insure that someone will become a social activist. Other social influences are needed to transform the belief about caring for others into action. This happened when Don moved to Denver and began teaching at a local college. This was his turning point.

> It was '66, the Vietnam War and the protests were heating up. One evening during freshman orientation week we were having a social for the new students and a young man came up and started chatting with me. And he finally asked, "What do you think about the Vietnam War?" I said: "Well, Lyndon Johnson says we're there to defend the South Vietnamese government and to help keep them safe from communism and give them a chance to be a democratic nation." Well, he started giving me all the facts about the past history of Vietnam, the French presence there, and how the U.S. took over after the French lost out, and he gave me stuff to read. So I started thinking about it and talking with him and gradually I began to feel that the U.S. really had no moral grounds for being there.

A few days later, the student he had met invited him to visit the office of the American Friends Service Committee in Denver. He learned about a peace vigil it sponsored and began to go each week at the appointed time and place. He also attended AFSC talks about timely social and political issues. Through these small steps, he was soon a committed peace activist.

> Looking back on it, I think the strong moral and ethical orientation in my life kind of came into play then because once I saw the war in ethical and moral terms, it seemed to me something that we shouldn't be involved in. So my whole background—my life as a young Catholic, as a seminarian, then as a priest—kind of clicked into place as I was faced with the social reality of the war.

Like many persisters, the Vietnam War forced Don to take a stand, and it had to be made in terms of his moral training. Once he was convinced the war was morally wrong, he was willing to take action. This decision—that some condition or policy violates a fundamental moral principle—is what moves people to abandon their settled lives for the uncertainty of protest.

David. A 39 year old persister, David became a peace activist by an unusual route, partly as a result of military service. During the 1960s, he grew up in a white, middle class suburb, led a rather sheltered life, went to a specialized technical college, and spent four years in the U.S. Air Force. He began to change his view of the military in college, where he was studying aerospace engineering. "I realized that, when I read the papers of the trade, most of the industry was intent on making killing machines for the military. And that kind of disillusioned me."

When he joined the Air Force, David was shocked by the way military literature addressed the use of nuclear weapons in "engineering language," with no moral sensitivity. The military way of life also offended him. He was appalled by the way the officers treated the men, not like adults but like children. "The pettiness and just plain stupidity of so much of it got me to rethinking my philosophy," he recalled.

After his military service, he became a flight instructor and found the "provincial, insular thinking of the military" present in civilian life as well. After instructing for two years, he came to a new realization on a cross-country bicycle trip.

> I had what is called a successful career. If you simply did what was expected of you and kept your nose clean, you got your promotions and pay raises regularly, whether it was in civilian life or military life. I realized that just about everything society was doing was destructive to the planet and to its own members. And I knew I was in a reorientation. I decided I was just going to do things that had meaning for me. I don't think I've been attached to an income since.

What is striking about the stories of these persisters is the gradual way that people evolve into persistent activists. There is no "identity crisis" which leads to a sudden conversion, a point James Hannon emphasizes in his life course view of peace commitment.[3] The evolution appears to be a gradual weaving together of socialization influences, social affiliations, the uniqueness of the historical moment, social criticism, and opportunities for action.

Hannon's findings, from his study of activists in the Pledge of

Resistance against U.S. military involvement in Central America, come closest to confirming our own. He emphasizes the influence of early religious socialization, with its accent on a utopian vision of society, a countercultural ethic, and a communitarian experience; the impact of the college experience as a radicalizing influence, which made people aware of social injustice; the influence of role models, who mentored others along radical lines; and the experience of being involved politically with like-minded others.

ETHICAL AND ACTIVIST IMPERATIVES

We have examined two aspects of peace socialization which were important in making our persisters available for career peace action. Their early training taught them to embrace the ethical imperative of living from deeply held moral principles, governing how people should treat one another and how they should live together in cooperation. As they witnessed the effects of war and of social injustice in the U.S. and abroad, they also adopted the activist imperative, expressed in the words: "It is my responsibility to change the world because it's the right thing to do."

When a person is motivated by ethical concerns and feels responsible for taking action, a shift in meaning occurs, away from the self-centered concerns of professional career and personal advancement toward the public good and common action. In Carmen Knudson-Ptacek's study, "Self Conceptions of Peace Activists,"[4] emphasis is placed on this shift of meaning. She found that peace activists experienced fulfillment and success through their relationships to others and saw their personal development evolving as they changed their orientation from self-interest to collective well-being. The sense of interdependence her respondents expressed reinforced their belief that they were responsible for solving global problems, that action had to take place cooperatively, and that they, themselves, were both the cause of the problem and the basis for its solution.

The four connections she discovered were the spiritual, a unified view of life which provided meaning and direction; the political, an understanding of how political processes work; the relational, friendship patterns which provided direct satisfaction as a result of bonding and the feeling of being personally committed to others; and the defensive, banding together for self-protection. The testimony of our respondents generally supports this line of thinking, for they spoke about these four connections at various times in relation to their commitment to the world community. They were clearly committed to this larger conception of obligation.

CONCLUSION

Overall, the stories of persisters revealed the importance of certain predisposing factors in preparing them for a peace career: They had developed beliefs about the need to help others, had become disenchanted with the political establishment, felt a strong sense of personal responsibility to work against violence and social injustice, and felt such work to be both useful and urgent. These predisposing factors are presented in Figure 2.1.

Figure 2.1: The Formation of an Attitudinal Predisposition

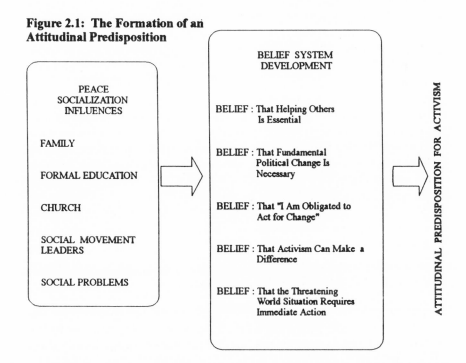

In the backgrounds of the ten people who left the movement, we found no clear differences between the early socialization influences which had initially predisposed them to become peace activists and those described by persisters. Some of those who left came from activist families, some from religious backgrounds which emphasized helping those in need, and others were brought to peace action by the Vietnam War and the civil rights movement. Some had all of those experiences. So, the character of the socialization influences which had led them to peace action offers little help in explaining why they eventually left. Later chapters will identify other factors which did make a difference.

It was surprising to discover a lack of uniformity in the early socialization experiences of our activists and such different combinations of social influences which shaped their preparation for peace careers. It was also interesting to learn that having an ethical belief about the need to care for others does not necessarily lead to activism, for many persisters embraced that principle but remained immersed in social quietism even into their adult years.

Our evidence suggests that political events are instrumental in activating a person's ethical core—their most strongly held beliefs. Until those core beliefs are mobilized, extended involvement in collective action is unlikely. This was why the protests of the 1960s and 1970s made such a difference; they touched the moral sensibilities of people to the point where they were willing to do something. In the heat of social protest, they were asked to take a stand. That meant their decision to become active, while motivated by their own moral concerns, was also strongly encouraged by the social pressures of the historical moment in which they lived. A perceived threat to one's life, to the lives of loved ones, or to the integrity of one's ethical beliefs activated the emotional energies of those who had been taught to "love your neighbor" in the abstract but who had not yet stepped across the line into collective action.

NOTES

1. Rick Suarez, Roger C. Mills, and Darlene Stewart, *Sanity, Insanity, and Common Sense.* (New York: Fawcett Columbine, 1987), p. 23.

2. Peter Berger and Thomas Luckman, *The Social Construction of Reality*. (New York: Doubleday, 1966).

3. James Hannon, "Becoming a Peace Activist: A Life Course Perspective," in Sam Marullo and John Lofland, eds., *Peace Action in the Eighties*. (New Brunswick, NJ: Rutgers University Press, 1990), pp. 217-232.

4. Carmen Knudson-Ptacek, "Self Conceptions of Peace Activists," in Marullo and Lofland, *op. cit.*, pp. 233-245.

3

AVAILABILITY AND OPPORTUNITY

Early socialization influences led many persisters to adopt beliefs that were in harmony with a peace action "calling." Together, those beliefs created an attitudinal readiness for peace activism, an important first step in the evolution of commitment. To transform this ideological inclination to act into action itself, the person had to become fully available for participation in the peace movement and opportunities for peace action had to be close at hand. As we will see, these two dimensions of commitment—availability and opportunity—interact closely with one another. These issues are explored in this chapter, as we shift our attention to the social and political contexts which stimulate the emergence of activism.

BECOMING AVAILABLE

We use availability as a concept to explore how free a person is to pursue a particular course of action.[1] While there are many factors which make a person freer to act, two are especially important. Attitude is crucial, where availability arises from the form of a person's beliefs, life experiences and depth of conviction. Is there a strong desire to take action because of personal beliefs and experiences? The activist's social situation is equally important, where the freedom to act hinges on the pattern of everyday life constraints. Given career and other pressing responsibilities, does the individual have the time and other resources to engage in peace action?

Attitudinal Availability

Attitudinal availability is based on the idea that a person becomes freer to pursue collective action because of a combination of beliefs and social experiences.[2] For example, an individual's experience within family, church, school, and among friends may have created so many peace-oriented beliefs that involvement in peace and social justice work becomes much more probable. Persisters often became available in this way, such as Jack, whose family and church experiences put him on such a clear path of activism in his youth that it has lasted over his lifetime.

Situational Availability

There are also people whose lives are designed in ways that make them freer for collective action. They may have more flexible careers, work part time, have no children, or do paid work in a peace organization. Their situation permits them to pursue their peace and social justice interests because they have more time and resources for it. David, who is a writer, falls into this category. Career flexibility allows him to attend peace organization meetings and to arrange his work schedule around his social movement obligations.

Responsibilities that compete with the peace movement for an activist's time and resources reduce that person's availability for movement work. For example, parents with children at home tend to have less time for peace action than those without parental responsibilities. However, having children can also strengthen commitment because they give their parents a powerful motivation to do peace work. Helen recalled a leader of the Rocky Flats Encirclement protest placing an enormous photograph of her 4 year old daughter in the rear window of her car urging demonstrators to "Do It For Emily."

Sometimes, other responsibilities become so demanding that activists must temporarily pull back from their peace efforts, usually returning when they have more time. Arlene remembered when she was "taking two classes at the university, working eight hours a day and because I didn't have the time, I dropped out of peace work for a couple of months." However, as soon as her obligations "lightened up, I got back in."

Life Designing

An individual will become fully available for peace action when peace-oriented beliefs have been developed and when time and other resources are in sufficient supply to make an activist commitment possible. Other factors may increase that availability: For example, when the individual perceives the world situation to be highly dangerous, or becomes closely associated with peace activists, or when society is in a dynamic phase of change and people are being asked to join protest movements. These and other factors increase the likelihood that a person with an ethical foundation for peace action will actually become involved. It is also important to note that availability is something which varies as a person's life situation changes, making for more or less freedom to act.

Once the step into peace action has been taken, availability expands further if the individual assumes an activist identity, taking on the activist role as part of life's meaning. When that identity is formed, often the corresponding feeling of a "peace mission" develops. The individual's activist identity and peace mission are reinforced by the personal investments and sacrifices required by the activist role, which also maintain that person's availability for peace activism. The more an individual contributes to a cause, the greater is the motivation to stay active in order to see the results.

Once the persisters developed an activist identity and sense of peace mission, situational availability was something they cultivated. They tended to structure their lives so as to be freer for peace action. An important dimension of designing availability was locating themselves within a local movement organization in order to be ready for action when the need arose. Where such organizations were absent or underdeveloped, persisters sometimes built them. Their direct involvement in organizational development put them in roles which increased their availability by requiring their time and energy. The crucial point is this: People whose beliefs compel them toward peace action become conscious creators of their own commitment by organizing their lives so they are freer to work for peace and social justice.

Persisters consciously sought to minimize demands that competed with obligations they felt toward their peace and social justice organizations. Some practiced voluntary simplicity, a way of life developed by counterculture groups in the 1970s. Their incomes were purposely kept below a taxable level, to reinforce a simple life style and to avoid contributing to government military expenditures. Their paid work schedules were kept flexible to insure availability for movement activities.

The kinds of food they ate, their housing arrangements, and their modes of transportation also reinforced their activist life style. Eating lower on the food chain, living in energy-efficient and cooperative housing, traveling by bicycle and public transportation—all encouraged full-time activism.

Some abandoned the idea of parenthood to ensure that they would have time for a full activist commitment. Others scheduled the births of their children and parenting responsibilities to harmonize with their movement obligations. Still others, like Rebecca, saw the parenting of children as part of their peace commitment. Besides her involvement in a women's peace collective, she put a substantial amount of peacemaking time into parenting and co-housing.

This conception of peace as including a broad range of life experiences and tasks encouraged full-time activism. Anything less than the complete integration of their personal lives with movement activities seemed to produce an uncomfortable dissonance for persisters. Uniting those two realms was one of their primary goals. They broadened their views of peace action so that their daily lives and movement work heavily overlapped. In this way, peace activism became inseparable from their everyday lives. This is why some of them talked about "living peace work," rather than merely doing it.

Another way some persisters designed their lives so movement work could be carried on was by choosing "significant others" (spouses, partners, housemates, and close friends) who shared their beliefs and political leanings. Members of an activist's personal network were often selected and retained in order to reinforce commitment, while those who might obstruct or weaken the resolve for peace action lost significance in an activist's life over time.

AVAILABILITY AND THE PERCEPTION OF NEED

To the extent that a pressing need for action was recognized, persisters maintained or increased their availability to serve. For many, this occurred in response to the threat of nuclear war or such crisis events as the Gulf War. Given the feeling of urgency, their ethical inclination to act and their place in local peace organizations led them to design their everyday lives so they had time to devote to movement work.

Sometimes an activist perceived a need in an entirely new area of action. For example, Helen decided to start a "city-twinning" project to fill a void she had discovered in the public's knowledge about the Russian people. She knew a great deal about nuclear weapons and felt the arguments against the arms race were compelling. People often agreed with her but would then ask: "But what about the Russians?" This question got her to thinking about how little she and others actually knew about the Russians. Helen set out to find a sister city in the Soviet Union for Boulder so that their citizens could learn more about each other. She thought this new knowledge would soften negative stereotypes and undermine the "enemy" mentality fueling the conflict between the two nations.

In other cases, the perceived need to act came from, as Michael put it, "circumstances in which some people feel they've got to do specific kinds of action to move things in a particular direction, or at least to stop things from going the way they are." This realization that action was necessary often emerged among these activists when an event strongly violated their sense of justice, or simply because someone "had to do it" given the fact that no one else was stepping forward, a finding Oliver's research supports.[3] This perception of the need to take action is often linked to what opportunities for action are present or can be created, a connection we will explore next.

THE OPPORTUNITY TO ACT

An activist's availability is transformed into action as a result of opportunity. "Opportunity" simply means that local peace groups and their targets for change are close enough at hand so that a person's willingness to become involved can be transformed into action. For example, there undoubtedly are some in the U.S. with peace-oriented beliefs who, because they are geographically isolated from peace movement activities, remain inactive. For persisters in the Denver-Boulder metropolitan area, there were many movement opportunities to pursue.

The concept of "opportunity structure" is applied in the collective action literature in a much more limited way than we use it. Elsewhere, theorists have used the term to explain broad structural changes in a political system which increase the possibility and tolerance for protest.[4] Here, the concept is expanded to include the different levels and contexts of opportunity within which the activist works.

Opportunity can mushroom during a period of heightened protest. This occurred in the 1960s and 1970s with the rise of the civil rights movement, the anti-Vietnam War movement, and the women's liberation movement. Each of these movements spawned hundreds of local protest groups, which provided new opportunities for action for millions of normally passive citizens. With these groups close by, many citizens participated in protest politics for the first time. In fact, most of our persisters were initially mobilized through one of those movements.

This national arena of activism was linked to a global culture of protest with clearly defined targets. In the 1980s, those targets of protest in the U.S. could not have been clearer. President Reagan's foreign policy, the U.S. and Soviet weapons buildup, and radiation pollution were seen as serious threats to humanity. At the same time, protests against governmental policy appeared to be increasingly effective in forcing policy changes, as had been demonstrated in the case of Vietnam. This was a global phenomenon as political systems from Poland to the Philippines seemed to become more responsive to protest politics. This spread of popular protest was the basis for a globally-based culture of nonviolent action, which has continued into the 1990s.

While policy makers in Washington were the primary target of protest movements, there were many local opportunities for activism where the targets were close at hand, visible, and perceived as dangerous. Such was the case of the Rocky Flats nuclear weapons plant. Its presence in the Denver-Boulder area stimulated protests for two decades. Many saw it as a menace to local public health and, given its nuclear weapons mission, also a threat to life on the planet. The prolonged protests at Rocky Flats suggest that proximity to a protest target can keep opportunities for action alive for years.

The large number of people with peace concerns living in the Denver-Boulder area also increased opportunity for those who were ready to enter activism. This heavy concentration of activists in metropolitan Denver increased the likelihood that people who were being drawn toward activism would make contact with others already involved, an important first step in commitment building. Starting a commitment, sustaining the culture of protest, building support networks, and reinforcing the idea of living for the movement were made easier by the sheer number of activists close to the protest targets.

Since Denver and Boulder already had well established peace organizations, people entering activism could either find opportunities within those organizations or more easily create new coalitions between them. The imaginative ways our activists exploited these organizational opportunities reveals much about how commitment is formed and sustained. Often, they reshaped their organizations for long-term survival, thereby insuring prolonged organizational opportunity for their own commitments. "I began to move into fund-raising and organizational support by putting a lot of my skills into that effort," Rebecca told us. "So I feel like I really gave the organization a base for starting their long-range planning and also established a funding system that was much more stable."

Together, the opportunities for protesting national policies, the easy access to local targets of protest, the high concentration of activists regionally and locally, and the presence and accessibility of local peace organizations gave persisters a broad array of opportunities for transforming their availability into action. The effect of those opportunities on the establishment of long-term commitment is what we turn to next.

Opportunities for Activism

Most of our activists developed their commitments to change during the 1970s and 1980s when restraints on protest against national policies were disappearing and new opportunities for activism were flourishing.

The National Scene. During the 1970s, the citizen who turned to social activism learned how to participate in everything from street politics to public policy hearings. The U.S. political system was being forced open by the challenges of its citizens. The credibility of the national government during that period was at a low point following its crises of Vietnam and Watergate. Activists were using every conceivable form of leverage, from environmental impact analyses to the Freedom of Information Act, to pry open the public policy process and make it responsive to protest pressure. By the 1980s, the larger political system had come to expect, tolerate, and even encourage this form of non-violent activism.

Most of our persisters had learned the basic skills of protest during the 1960s and 1970s and were ready to refine them into a continuing activist role in the 1980s. Reagan administration policies which emphasized the rebuilding and rededication of military institutions, large increases in military spending, tough talk from the President to Soviet leaders, military repression and intervention in Latin America provided prominent new targets for peace activists.

The Cold War expansion of the military and nuclear industrial complexes throughout the nation had, by the 1980s, provided the peace movement with ample evidence of the military and environmental threats posed by those installations in their communities. Those installations were seen as seriously aggravating societal and global problems rather than ensuring national security. As Jonathan put it: "It's all connected, it's all part of the same system which puts profit and money before humanity and working out the problems."

Local Opportunities. National movements, such as the civil rights movement, the anti-war movements, and the women's liberation movement, served to make persistent activism more likely because they raised important ethical contradictions that were deeply rooted in the societal structure. However, it was in the local communities where peace activists worked that those broader national and global problems were translated into immediate opportunities for peace and social justice work.

Opportunities for peace action in Metropolitan Denver in the 1970s and 1980s were numerous. The area was a theater of action designed for a morality play. The evil installations of war were all around: Rocky Flats, the Rocky Mountain Arsenal, Lowry Air Force Base, Martin Marietta, with a second great concentration of military activity in Colorado Springs not far to the south. As a regional federal center, Denver also hosted the large administrative buildings which became leading targets of public protest.

There were large numbers of peace-attentive citizens ready to be mobilized, first into consensus communities, as Klandermans might call them, then into direct action.[5] There was also a dense network of peace and environmental organizations, whose interests often converged on issues like the closing of Rocky Flats, which were ready to mobilize that consensus and readiness for action. In short, available peace activists did not lack opportunity. As McCarthy and Zald might put it, peace action entrepreneurs in the 1980s were working in a growth industry.[6]

Accessible Targets of Protest. The importance of the physical presence of military installations cannot be overstated as a commitment-making factor. Having the physical manifestation of an abstract threat in one's community strengthens the perception of the need to act and encourages the commitment to do so. The presence of Rocky Flats, for example, with the migration of its plutonium releases downwind and downstream from the plant, right across Denver, made the threat impossible to ignore. Thus, it is not surprising that so many of our activists mentioned Rocky Flats as a major influence in the formation of their commitments. In fact, some of our respondents built their peace careers largely around that single installation. For instance, Don spent several years focusing on the issues surrounding the plant and, even after weapons production there ended, he was still involved with its workers' and nuclear waste issues.

Military installations were theaters of protest for the public presentation of peace issues. The Rocky Flats site, where nuclear bomb triggers were being manufactured, and the federal courthouse, where the more recalcitrant demonstrators were held, tried, and sentenced, became stages for dramatic protests. Events such as The Rocky Flats Encirclement—a fifteen-mile chain of demonstrators holding hands around the plant perimeter in an act of solidarity for peace—required months of preparation. It provided peace organizers with a compelling focus for mobilizing peace sympathizers for longer term commitments.

Such demonstrations had an especially important effect on long-term activists. They solidified the peace community, secured a renewal of commitment from activists, and permitted them to perform their roles in public and to practice their "front stage" skills: Public relations work, front line organizing, and nonviolence training for the marshals who were responsible for keeping the thousands of protesters faithful to the principle of nonviolence.

For persistent activists, these public protests were opportunities for presentation of self in a setting where a common definition of the situation, as Goffman would say, validated the role of the career peace activist.[7] The officials ready to negotiate, the media eager to record, the audience waiting to listen—all confirmed the value and effectiveness of what peace activists were spending their lives doing.

Mass demonstrations at Rocky Flats have been viewed elsewhere through a dramaturgical lens.[8] Through that perspective, it is clear why movement activists need to publicly confront their opponents at regular intervals. Such a dramatic presentation of the conflict reaffirms the activist's identity in relationship to the targets of change. It provides an audience for that reaffirmation, including those physically present as well as others who are reached by the mass media.

The Need for Community. To flourish, persisters need a more intimate community of committed activists drawn from the larger peace-attentive population, where their long-term commitments to peace and social justice can be supported and encouraged. Without this group solidarity, persistent activism is just too lonely an enterprise and too discouraging. All of our activists worked to build that sense of community. Some, like Sally, invested large amounts of time in the effort. "My main commitment the first couple of years was to the Communities Project, writing this book on community and developing community."

As noted earlier, Boulder as the home of a major university and Denver as a cultural and political center provided a substantial population of peace-attentive people. This made it easier for persisters to find others of similar persuasion and to build a "critical mass" of people whose beliefs and solid footing in the peace community could help activists "keep the faith" and continue the work.

Organizational Density and Diversity. Another major component of an activist's immediate structure of opportunity is organizational density, the existence of many groups working for peace and social justice in an area and, consequently, the presence of diverse projects and actions to choose from. While the needs of these activists varied, most felt that, to claim their loyalty, a peace organization needed to do two things. It had to be working for system-wide change and it had to offer them a niche, preferably for the long-term, where they could "live out their values" in creative ways.

Persisters were looking for a comfortable working environment in a peace organization that reflected their own goals for social change and their desire for consensual decision-making. They were more likely to find such organizations where the broader community was densely populated with peace activists and where various types of peace groups were present. The Denver-Boulder area offered that density and diversity.

Three types of organizations were present in the metropolitan area for peace activists who were ready to make a lifetime commitment. There were secular groups, such as the Rocky Mountain Peace Center, which were trying to eliminate violence by working for major societal changes. Such groups provided a wide range of program opportunities to activists as well as organizational flexibility. With this flexibility, there was an increased chance that an organization would develop the capacity to survive. This potential staying power seemed important to some activists, like Allen, who was partly attracted to the Rocky Mountain Peace Center because "it's been around a while, so it's working on a tradition. We need to have groups where somebody's going to be concerned about what just hit the paper yesterday and be educated and sophisticated enough to tie its issues together."

Religious organizations with a definable peace testimony, such as Quaker, Mennonite, Brethren and Catholic peace and social justice groups, were also well-represented among those organizations our activists joined. The faith-based emphasis of these groups gave activists like Grant a way to serve their religious communities through their interests in peace and social justice. He and his wife had moved to Denver "looking for an opportunity to do a full-time peace-making ministry. We had our room and board and basic needs provided for and spent two years as volunteer staff." Prior to that move, they had been working for peace and social justice in a rural state, but became frustrated by the resistance of members of their congregation to those concerns and by their isolation from other Christian activists. By moving to an urban area, their hope was to make contact with others of their faith who, like them, had realized the importance of social change as part of the Christian mission.

A third type of organization persisters themselves created. Attracted to a particular issue, they sometimes developed organizations from scratch or made connections between single-issue peace and social justice groups to forge coalitions. They welcomed the opportunities this organization-building provided for applying their skills and developing something new out of their own inspiration.

Finding the Right Movement Organization

Our activists maintained their availability by joining peace organizations whose goals and ways of working were similar to their own. They were attracted to organizations which offered opportunities for the kind of peace action they wanted to pursue and provided them with a collective identity in harmony with their beliefs. Some found that identity in pacifist religious groups like the Quakers, Mennonites, and radical Catholics, each of which is at the center of a supporting network of individuals. This suggests the central importance of social networks as catalysts for identity and commitment. Other research has noted this. For example, Melucci shows how collective identity develops among movement members within their social networks.[9] Snow, Zurcher and Ekland-Olson's work on recruitment to social movements emphasizes the significance of voluntary associations, such as civic clubs, in recruiting movement membership.[10] Their findings confirm the observations of Gerlach and Hine about the positive influence of social networks on commitment generally.[11] Likewise, the significance of counter-cultural networks in making people available for movement activity is illustrated in Kriesi's work on Dutch peace action.[12]

Persisters were also attracted to particular organizations for reasons other than identity. Some were drawn toward leaders in the organization. Martha had become involved with Hull House in Chicago in the 1920s because of its director, Jane Addams. Others, like Don, were impressed by the day-to-day workers who keep an organization going. He found them "very welcoming, very committed and knowledgeable people, who were doing things that seemed important to me, like draft counseling and educational programs. My feeling was that they were very committed."

Others were attracted by the status of a group's members in the community, because it might strengthen the organization's potential impact. Philip was attracted to the Colorado Coalition because of the diverse and articulate people who were involved, people with resources that could help keep the organization going. This peace group interested him because it had the main characteristics he was looking for, a group with "staying power" and "the ability to influence the way the issue was presented and dealt with in the public eye."

Given the importance of beliefs in building commitment, many persisters were attracted to organizations because of their ideological orientation and goals. Sally was attracted to the group she eventually joined because it was oriented to long-term structural changes in society and not just "fixing things up" in a cosmetic way.

How decisions were made and how authority was structured were also important for some persisters in choosing an organization to join. Since they sought a vehicle for their longer term development as activists, they wanted an organization where they could participate fully in decisions and where they would have some autonomy in creating meaningful roles for themselves. Many became involved in organizations because of this opportunity for inventiveness. For example, Matt joined an organization to pursue an imaginative project that used his writing skills, his fluency in Spanish, and his enthusiasm for migrant labor justice.

Matt and a few others were also attracted by paid positions in organizations appearing to have the capacity for effectiveness, positions that promised long-term potential for making a difference while getting paid for it. Being able to make a modest living from their peace work was seen by them as a rare privilege.

The stability provided by paid work in an organization, while it was important, was sometimes less significant than the kind of work they were able to do over long periods of time. The depth and continuity of a project attracted Jonathan, who was heavily involved in actions to close down the nuclear weapons plant at Rocky Flats. This included protesting the imprisonment of a co-activist.

> I vigiled first once a week, then twice a week, and then daily for up to two years, habitually in front of the Federal Courthouse about the

railroading of Jennifer Haynes being sent to the federal penitentiary. There was a lot of hostility toward me from others and over time, individually, people would at least be willing to dialogue.

A number of persisters joined a particular peace organization because they just felt they belonged there. There was an immediate feeling of community. As Suzanne put it, "when I went there I discovered that I felt comfortable. They were people that I felt some kinship with."

It was common for persisters to be drawn to or create movement organizations which promised intimacy, informality, and community. They wanted to work with a small, democratic team of like-minded people where there was a lot of project flexibility. Susan's branch of Peace Action had this loose-knit quality. It was a handful of people who were doing canvassing from door to door to convince people about the need for a nuclear weapons freeze. Working democratically and toward consensus, about nine people were jointly responsible for deciding what they would do as an organization. They were in it together as equals.

"Connection" was another theme which emerged in our activists' accounts of what made them likely to join particular organizations. They looked especially for a personal tie to an organization's analysis and approach to social problems. For some, like Brian, this connection occurred around personal identity and other relevant issues. The New Jewish Agenda gave him the opportunity to "express my activism in terms of my Jewish identity. What attracted me to that group was this notion of asserting an alternative Jewish identity because I feel a special responsibility as a Jew to work on behalf of Palestinian rights." For Grant, the connection was primarily between his religious faith and the peace issues he felt his church had neglected.

> I was convinced that justice and peacemaking were central to the faith and to the Gospel and I felt strongly that the church had neglected or even betrayed the centrality of peacemaking, non-violence and concern for justice. I wanted to lift up this concern for the faith community. I was not as interested in being involved in a strictly politically oriented group. I really wanted to challenge my faith community, so it was always important for me to be involved with groups that had a faith orientation.

The reasons persisters gave for being attracted to an organization were what made them want to devote their time and energy to its goals and projects. As long as it met their expectations and remained faithful to a work style and activities that were in harmony with their own beliefs and preferences, they found ways to maintain their availability for the work.

Creativity

Embracing peace-oriented beliefs, persisters shaped their lives and positioned themselves so they could fully exploit their personal opportunity structures. They not only responded to various opportunities presented to them, but they consciously invented their own. This process suggests a greater creative role for activists, in the way their commitments form and persist, than has been suggested in the social movements literature.

This creative impulse was shown in the way these activists cultivated and used their opportunities in local peace groups. They were often drawn to challenging tasks within strategic organizations where they felt the action was. But that action could take diverse forms and proceed at different paces. Some, like Beth, found nonviolent direct action, like the Nevada Test Site campaign, to be especially important.

> I started at the Rocky Mountain Peace Center by working with the Nevada Test Site Protest. Actually, a friend put me on to it. He asked me to do the press work for a group which was going to infiltrate the test site and try to sit on top of Ground Zero and stop nuclear testing. I got really hooked on that and I had just quit my job so I had a lot of time. I worked as a volunteer with the Peace Center to help send teams which were going to hike onto the test site. I went to Nevada and provided support to groups in Las Vegas and at the site.

When opportunities for action disappear, lose their challenge or their capacity to directly confront a target for change, some activists may become disillusioned and leave. For example, Allen had been drawn to the Rocky Mountain Peace Center by the opportunity to make a difference. He proposed and then was hired to lead a Central America solidarity project which organized civil disobedience against the U.S. government's role in Central America and offered programs to educate the public about it. One of the most widely publicized actions of the project was a caravan to El Salvador, which included 30 people, 13 trucks, and 20 tons of medicine and tools. That was his last movement effort, for he left activism soon after the supplies were delivered. Helen's exit from activism followed a similar course.

After the ceremony establishing the sister city relationship, with the visiting officials on their way back to the Soviet Union, she resigned from her leadership position. Not long thereafter, she left peace activism.

These two people who dropped out of activism, at least temporarily, perceived a need and seized an interesting opportunity, meeting it with imagination and total commitment. But there was little readiness to go on to other movement work when finished with their tasks. Their commitments seemed to revolve around issues rather than the life of the peace movement as a whole.

In contrast, persisters seemed more attentive to movement-tending and building. Jonathan's attention to maintaining the Rocky Flats protest over many years illustrates the patience and commitment of movement-nurturing.

> I plant and water the peace garden regularly, go to the vigils every Sunday regardless of the weather, go to Rocky Flats monitoring council meetings, help develop allies and demonstrations, and go to court hearings to support people who are very active out there.

Others, such as Pauline, became movement builders. After her position in solar energy research was eliminated, she began to look around to "see what I could most usefully do with my life." She began to go to arms control meetings where she discovered the need for a coalition of citizens who could take that issue to mainstream audiences. She gathered a number of people together who agreed with her that a coalition was needed. They proceeded carefully, first by finding a lawyer who was willing to draft their by-laws and apply for tax exempt status, then methodically screening the names of prominent citizens with "a lot of credibility from all aspects of the community" for "a coalition that was going to focus on talking to middle America." When coalition recruitment was completed, they spent many hours gathering information about the issues and deciding on strategy, so they could address arms control intelligently and effectively.

Connecting elements of the movement for greater effectiveness and continuity was Pauline's special contribution to movement-building. She became available, identified a goal, then set about the task of realizing it. Her work supports the theoretical notion that collective action is an extension of conventional politics, rationally approached. It also shows how creativity, free time, personal location in social networks and movement or-ganizations, perception of the need to act, and the wish to be useful all combine with an activist's beliefs to bring availability and opportunity together.

If there are changes in personal availability or opportunities, activists may shift their action focus, leave one organization or movement for another, or quit activism entirely. Some activists respond to changes in life situation, such as a career shift, by moving into a related movement. Such moves are made easier when a person's beliefs encompass nonviolence as it is broadly defined. Believing in nonviolence as a life style, or as the appro-priate ethic for carrying on human relationships, makes it pos-sible for someone to be a peace activist in a number of related movements not specifically devoted to peace action.

This kind of flexibility tends to encourage the persistence of activism, not necessarily within a single movement, but through work in several movements simultaneously. In fact, some of these activists appeared to be "nodes" of activism, connecting various movements together around the issues of peace, the en-vironment, women's issues, and economic justice. June's activism, for example, linked the movements for peace, women's rights and good government.

CONCLUSION

Availability and opportunity interact to encourage persistent activism. In Figure 3.1, we show how, as their peace commit-ments reached a certain level of development, these peace workers adopted the identity, status, and role of career activist.

They maintained their availability for peace action through their continuing involvement in movement organizations over long periods and by consciously designing their everyday lives so they were free to pursue movement work. This put them in a state of readiness to respond to opportunities when they presented themselves.

Opportunities for collective action develop at the national and global levels as political and economic events and trends present new possibilities for protest politics, in what has been called the political opportunity structure. That system-wide structure of opportunity for action produces a personal structure of oppor-tunity for each activist, who exploits it while developing and refining the activist role. The experience of our activists reveals

Figure 3.1: Availability and Opportunity for Activism

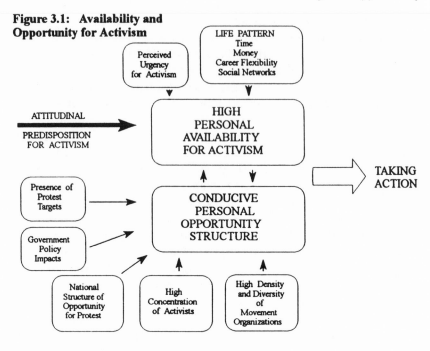

the importance of organizational flexibility and continual personal reassessment of their activism in the development of sustained commitment. For such "purposive change professionals," the range of peace issues must be broad enough and the vision of nonviolent social relations sufficiently inclusive to enable them to persist in peace action.

NOTES

1. Availability and opportunity are concepts explored in depth in James V. Downton, Jr., *Rebel Leadership: Commitment and Charisma in the Revolutionary Process*. (New York: The Free Press, 1973); *Sacred Journeys: The Conversion of Young Americans to Divine Light Mission*. (New York: Columbia University Press, 1979); and "Spiritual Conversion and Commitment: The Case of Divine Light Mission," *Journal for the Scientific Study of Religion*, 19 (1980), pp. 381-396.

2. Attitudinal availability is related to the notion of biographical availability developed by Doug McAdam, "The Biographical Consequences of Activism," *op. cit.*, pp. 744-760. He appears to use biographical

availability to refer to both past life experience and present life structure determinants that render an activist available to a movement. We use attitudinal availability only in reference to former life experience, terming the latter situational availability.

3. Pamela Oliver, "If You Don't Do It, Nobody Will: Active and Token Contributors to Local Collective Action," *American Sociological Review*, 49 (1984), pp. 601-610.

4. For different approaches to this concept see: Doug McAdam, *Political Process and the Development of Black Insurgency, 1930-1970*. (Chicago: University of Chicago Press, 1982); Peter Eisinger, "The Conditions of Protest Behavior in American Cities," *American Political Science Review*, 67 (1973), pp. 11-28; Sidney Tarrow, *Democracy and Disorder: Society and Politics in Italy, 1965-1975*. (Oxford: Oxford University Press, 1988).

5. Bert Klandermans, "The Formation and Mobilization of Consensus," in Klandermans, Kriesi and Tarrow, *op. cit.*, pp. 173-196.

6. The concept of social movement entrepreneurship is developed in John McCarthy and Mayer Zald, "Resource Mobilization and Social Movements: A Partial Theory," *American Journal of Sociology*, 82 (1977), pp. 1212-1241.

7. Erving Goffman, *Presentation of Self in Everyday Life*. (New York: Doubleday Anchor, 1959).

8. Paul Wehr, *Conflict Regulation*. (Boulder, CO: Westview Press, 1979), pp. 101-122.

9. Alberto Melucci, "Getting Involved: Identity and Mobilization in Social Movements," in Klandermans, Kriesi and Tarrow, *op. cit.*, pp. 329-348.

10. David Snow, Louis Zurcher, Jr. and Sheldon Ekland-Olson, "Social Networks and Social Movements: A Microstructural Approach to Differential Recruitment," *American Sociological Review*, 45 (1980), pp. 787-801.

11. Luther Gerlach and Virginia Hine, *People, Power and Change: Movements of Social Transformation*. (Indianapolis: Bobbs-Merrill, 1970).

12. Hanspeter Kriesi, "Local Mobilization for the People's Petition of the Dutch Peace Movement," in Klandermans, Kriesi and Tarrow, *op. cit.*, pp. 41-82.

4

DEVELOPING COMMITMENT

Many persisters became available for activism through their early socialization experiences and because they organized their lives for peace action. They were free to develop an activist commitment at a time when opportunities for protest were abundant. Many groups were mobilizing to end the war in Vietnam, to close military installations like Rocky Flats, to change U.S. policy in Latin America, and to improve relations with the Soviet Union to reduce the threat of nuclear war.

The 1960s, 1970s and 1980s were decades of social activism, as thousands of normally passive citizens turned their energies to social change. Most were short-term activists who eventually returned to conventional careers, but some entered activism to stay. Those were the persisters who developed a commitment that would last. How that commitment formed is the focus of this chapter.

COMMITMENT AND BONDING

In "Notes on the Concept of Commitment," Howard Becker abandoned the then prevailing view of commitment as a subjective state of mind in favor of a behavioral definition of the concept as "a consistent line of action."[1] How committed an individual is can be determined, he argues, by observing how consistently a particular course of action is pursued. This behavioral perspective of commitment is useful in the study of collective action because it leads to an examination of how consistently participants conform to the ethical principles, social norms, and goals of the movement they have joined.

It is important to note that allegiance, a consequence of social bonding, is extended by the activist not only to the movement as a whole, but also to its ideology (beliefs), organization, leadership, and to the movement community at large (its social network). These are important sectors of a movement the individual may bond to through commitment.[2]

In looking at an individual's commitment, it is important to notice the social sectors from which that commitment receives its strength, the relative depth of the bonding to each sector, and its waxing and waning as a result of changing circumstances. Bonds can strengthen or weaken because of changes which occur within the movement organization and in the individual's broader life situation. Therefore, a person's commitment is apt to fluctuate in intensity. In fact, as the cases of our shifters and dropouts will show, when a bond with one of these sectors is broken, the result may be a fairly quick exit from the group.

Most persisters described themselves as being strongly or very strongly committed to peace and social justice causes, while a few had weaker commitments dictated by advancing age. At various points in their peace careers, all persisters had been strongly committed. These self-assessments of commitment strength were borne out by the amount of time they spent in peace and social justice work. Most worked from 10 to 60 hours a week on those issues, many also having to work elsewhere to support themselves and their families. When an important action was under way, the number of hours they devoted to peace action soared.

Many were also willing to put themselves on the line in terms of arrest and imprisonment. Eighty-five year old Martha tells the story of how, with a good friend, she was arrested at a Rocky Flats demonstration.

> We crawled under the fence and laid down on our raincoats. The goons picked us up and carried us to a place to get fingerprinted. They had a woman put on rubber gloves and check to see if we had drugs. They put us in manacles, waist chains and leg irons. They took us down to the women's prison because there's no Denver jail for women. So, we had an interesting time in the cells with the ladies of the night.

Shifters and dropouts also reported that their involvement had been extensive while they were active members of the peace movement. So, the level of involvement did not help to explain why they eventually shifted their commitment or dropped out.

However, bonding issues were important in accounting for the erosion of their commitment.

Bonding to the Ideology

Most persisters felt their beliefs were compatible with those of their peace organizations. Furthermore, they were aware of sharing the same beliefs with others in the peace community. This created a high level of ideological agreement, which strengthened their commitment. What were some of the important beliefs they shared?

There was a strong commitment to nonviolence and democracy. Michael talked about the importance of these issues. For him, nonviolence encompassed an attitude of respect for others and the willingness to take a risk to stop violence. Democracy included self-rule and self-determination, "where all people are participating in the decisions that affect them."

Persisters also resisted hierarchical social arrangements, based on their commitment to the principles of nonviolence and equality. Lynn's comment captured the general sentiment.

> A lot of my beliefs are incorporated in nonviolent principles and this includes creating non-hierarchical structures. I really believe in equal relationships, that people have a sort of equal accessibility to whatever is here. In the house where I live, it's important for me to live at approximately the level our homeless guests are living at. It's important to me that people be aware that racism and sexism are not acceptable in our life together.

Many persisters believed that people have no right to more than they need and the less fortunate should not be denied their share. Helping those in need was a widely held goal. Martha captured this idea when she said: "I think it's wrong to hurt other people, and I think it's right to try to help people that need help. So that's it."

Most persisters believed in self-realization, people having the right to develop as individuals without societal limitations, while they also strongly supported personal responsibility between people and toward the earth. They firmly believed in diversity, respecting differences between individuals, their various points of view and diverse life styles. Grant saw this as part of the task of "accepting personal responsibility for my life and the way it affects other people." He felt that "our lives and welfare are connected," so we need to respect and care for each other. This common welfare is closely connected to environmental issues, for many persisters also expressed the belief that people should take personal responsibility for living with the earth in a more sustainable way.

Among the more religious, there was a belief in the divinity of people, an intangible but precious inner spirit which needed to be honored. They might have agreed with Jack.

> Each human being is divine. There's a divine light in each person and that is of the highest importance and should be cultivated, respected, and nourished. We should not encourage mayhem or death, shortening people's lives, limiting their quality of life, or interfering with their ability to develop that divinity within them.

Persisters also believed that people should take action to correct the many injustices in the world and to work for peace between nations and peoples, based on the Christian principle, "Love your neighbor as yourself." Susan expressed this principle when she said: "You've got to treat people right and that includes animals and kids too."

Among shifters and dropouts, there were two who left in part because their bonding to their group's ideology had weakened to a point where they felt they could no longer be members. Their cases will be discussed in the next section.

Bonding to the Organization

Most persisters felt bonded to their peace organizations, generally approving of what they were doing and how they were being run. They also felt that the organization's principles reflected their own. Thus, overall, there was a feeling of satisfaction with their movement groups.

Persisters were drawn to their peace organizations partly because those groups were pursuing courses of action with which they generally agreed. June described how her peace organizations embraced what was of value to her. This did not mean that she always agreed with them on specific issues, but that generally she felt comfortable with their goals and how they operated day-to-day.

When an organization's principles or policies diverged sharply from the beliefs or preferences of an activist, the resulting conflict was sometimes sufficient to break that person's bond to the organization. For example, Beth became alienated from her peace group because its governing board took what she regarded as an inappropriate stand on principle in a case of sexual exploitation of women in the community by a man in a position of authority. She was also frustrated that her group had not become more involved in the broader issue of the abuse of women and children. The conflict between the organization's position and her own beliefs eventually led her to leave the group and to redirect her energies toward ending domestic violence. Although she is no longer directly involved in the peace movement, she sees this change as a continuation of her peace and social justice work.

Most persisters felt their organizations were running well, although some had minor criticisms. Their overall impression was that their organizations were structured around beliefs they agreed with and that they functioned quite well by those beliefs. The organizations did not have to be perfect for them to be satisfied, as long as there was a sincere effort to resolve conflicts and to eliminate the problems.

While persisters sometimes criticized specific policies or the way their organizations functioned at the national or regional level, they appreciated the participatory nature of the decision-making process. Arlene characterized her peace group as "very democratic. We try to reach consensus, but generally fall back on majority rule. There's rarely a time when there's a fight over what we're doing. I think we're pretty open with each other, and it goes along pretty well."

The democratic nature of such peace organizations, with their emphasis on consensus decision-making, shared leadership, open communication, and equality sets them off from conventional movement organizations. It is the basis for the feeling of satisfaction persisters expressed about their organizations. There could be problems, even severe ones, but the organization's effort to operate according to the principles of participatory democracy, cooperation, and empowerment tended to preserve their bonds with it. Specific failures of the organization or disagreements with its handling of a particular situation could be forgiven. In fact, most persisters realized that, given the participatory nature of their organizations, more conflict than usual was to be expected. Brian understood this. After complaining about "quarreling" and "gossip" in his organization, he added: "I guess ultimately I'd have to say that I wouldn't try to make any major changes because as inefficient as participatory democracy is as a method, that's what we're all committed to."

Most shifters and dropouts also expressed satisfaction with the peace groups they had been involved with, although, as noted above, Beth left her organization over principle. Her case demonstrates the importance of bonding to an organization as a condition for maintaining commitment. When that bond is broken and cannot be repaired, exit is often only a matter of time.

Bonding to Leadership

Most persisters felt the leaders of their groups were effective and dedicated, although judgments varied from "excellent" to "okay." Grant was among those who had a positive impression. "In the groups I'm involved in, I think that the leadership is doing an excellent job." Others were equally laudatory, but often the praise was mixed with an awareness of shortcomings, that leaders were not always effective. "They make mistakes," Jack noted, "but they learn from them generally and they're gentle in undoing their mistakes and resentment is not usually carried about."

While persisters had some criticisms, overall they felt positive about their leaders, although there was a tendency not to express feelings of personal loyalty to them. Given the strong emphasis in peace groups on equality, personal loyalty to leadership was discouraged in order to avoid hierarchy. "There is a sense of personal loyalty among people certainly," Brian said, "but in terms of leaders and followers there's nothing like that, at least I hope not."

Even with this subtle prohibition, some persisters did feel a sense of selective loyalty, given to some leaders and not others. Many, though, felt no personal loyalty to leaders at all, but still remained committed for reasons Joan described.

> In this particular group, I don't feel loyalty to the leader. What I feel loyal to is the group itself, the mission of the group and the organization as a whole. I don't feel personal loyalty to the person who's in charge. My loyalty to the group is really what keeps my commitment going.

Joan's view shows the importance of factors other than a personal bond to leadership which keep an individual's commitment intact. But, among those who felt good about their leaders, a sense of personal loyalty to them tended to strengthen those positive feelings. Even those who were sometimes critical of their leaders were not sufficiently dissatisfied with them to leave.

Only in Monica's case was disappointment with a leader cause for leaving. She left because she was unhappy with the arbitrary authority wielded by a key leader of her group. "The Executive Director was an unpaid full-time staff person who saw herself as being in charge. She literally scripted the demonstrations to the point where she'd get very angry if a person stepped outside of the script for even a minute."

Monica's criticism was not only of this arbitrary leadership, but of the organization's structure, a clearly defined hierarchy which encouraged a more conventional leadership style. So, although exit from her peace group was prompted by the autocratic style of its director, her disillusionment arose from a conflict over principle with the group itself. Valuing participatory democracy, she could not stay in a peace organization which seemed to put so little stock in it.

There were two functions leaders performed for our activists. One was running the organization; another was symbolic, as certain leaders were identified by persisters as exemplars of peace and social justice activism. Sometimes leaders played both organizational and symbolic roles, but not always.

Organizational leaders were admired by persisters for their fair-mindedness, their commitment to running the organization in a democratic way, and their effort to live in harmony with other principles persisters considered core beliefs. Symbolic leaders were valued in a different way, not so much for their organizational abilities, although many were good organizers, but for who they had become as people. They were admired for their persistence as peace activists, for enduring hardship (such as going to prison), for their commitment to principle rather than results, for their willingness to live and not just speak their commitment.

When asked which dedicated peace activists had influenced their own activism, most of our respondents identified individuals in their own organizations. There were references to

Gandhi, Jane Addams, Martin Luther King, Jr., Philip Berrigan, Thomas Merton, and Dorothy Day, but, generally, more attention was given to local leaders. The lives of these local community leaders were examples of how to engage in activism: How to behave, how to act, how to persist, and how to maintain a sense of integrity about the work. Don offered this perspective.

> One learns from people like that about how to really create change. They're an inspiration. You see them giving their life to this cause and not getting a lot out of it financially and often working hard and long hours and not getting much satisfaction. So, I guess it's the example, inspiration, and the concrete things you learn from them.

They were examples, but they were more than that. They also served as pivotal points for community. Despite the emphasis on equality in most peace groups, certain people were elevated by these activists as inspirations for community and individual effort. They helped others to focus on right action, not on results. Helen learned this lesson from two local peace activists she felt were inspirational leaders.

> Those men really lived the belief that you did things because they were the right things to do and you didn't look at the results, because as soon as you look at the results, you tend to rush the work, you know, get hysterical about it, become more radical than you need to be. And I really believe that's how the work has to be done. It has to be done carefully, thoroughly, and honestly. We need to push as much as possible, but be constant, calm, and focused on what is the right thing to do.

These local leaders exemplified not only perseverance for our respondents, but the integrity of peace activism when it flows from higher principles and not from egoism (with its tendency toward anger, impatience, and competition).

People who shifted to other movements and those who dropped out of activism also had local leaders who inspired them, but this was not sufficient to keep them committed. Counteracting forces were stronger, like Beth's disillusionment with her peace organization and Monica's with an autocratic leader.

Bonding to the Community

The idea of community is a social creation. People use this term to refer to something they want to create or have created.

Community as an idea captures a complex set of relationships among people involved in an on-going activity together. Given those relationships, people say "I'm part of a community" or "There is a real feeling of community here."

What relationships need to exist for people to perceive that community exists? Among persisters, the following were important: Embracing a common vision of social change; sharing similar principles, the struggle, and the work; giving support to people who needed it; being able to receive support offered by others, feeling cared about, having close personal friendships in the community; and sharing experiences with other members of the community over a long period.

At its heart, a sense of community revolves around the issue of belonging. Do people feel that they are a part of the group? Belonging is partly based on how much is shared with other members in terms of principles, adversity and good times. Normally, we think of community as either existing or not; we fail to consider the differing experiences with community that members have. The more one shares with others, the stronger the feeling of community; the less one shares, the weaker that feeling is likely to be. People who work in an organization will feel different degrees of community based on how much they share with others at any moment in time. In short, community is not a static thing. It changes as circumstances alter what is held in common by a group's members. When engaged in a protracted struggle against a specific war or nuclear facility, for example, the sense of community may expand to include many people. It will deepen as those people spend many hours together, organizing and then participating in demonstrations, getting arrested, going to jail, being arraigned and going through the subsequent court process. When there is no common, dramatic focus for the energies of peace activists, the sense of community may temporarily wane, as people return to other pressing matters in their lives.

For persisters, a sense of community developed with close friends in their movement organizations and with nonmovement friends who supported their activism. The vast majority described having strong personal ties with others. Most would have agreed with Rebecca: "Almost all the people I care to spend any time with are in the movement in some way."

Having close friends in the movement gave persisters a sense of belonging which affected their commitment. Diane felt that, without a sense of belonging, "it would be hard to stay in the movement." This feeling of closeness to others who are also working to change the world creates a home for the persister. It is secure, nurturing, loving, and it becomes a foundation for the work. In fact, creating community can become as important as specific peace projects. "When I first got involved in peace activism," Grant recalled, "my commitment came out of a sense of righteousness and my friendships grew out of a cause. Now, my commitment flows more from my search for community."

Close friendships are the heart of community, forged by countless hours of working together. They are created out of common sacrifices, of organizing and participating in demonstrations, giving each other support during discouraging times, laughing, praying and struggling over decisions together, facing victory and defeat together. Susan emphasized this.

> Friendship is one of the things that keeps me going, just the encouragement and support of people. Those are some of my strongest friendships because you go through a lot together. I've had handcuffs on with these people and I've marched in the streets with them.

These experiences of friendship "in the trenches" are what bring community into being. As people make close friends within the movement, their political and social lives become more integrated, which has the effect of strengthening community and commitment. "When your social life gets mixed up with your political work," Brian told us, "that kind of ties you into it more strongly."

While this sense of community based on close friendships definitely strengthened the commitment of most persisters, there was one exception. David was more socially isolated: "I'm what you call a loner. I can't honestly say that I've ever had intimate friends in my life. In most gatherings, I'm not exactly the life of the party and not very social." Yet, he was strongly committed to peace and social justice work. Having embraced peace-oriented beliefs and an activist identity, he remained committed even though he did not feel closely tied to the peace community.

David's case suggests that peace-oriented beliefs may be a sufficient condition for peace activism, while being integrated into the community may not. Yet, a feeling of community seems to reinforce beliefs as well as the person's sense of responsibility to act on them, and it offers hope that something can be accomplished. "Without a community you end up being real isolated and it doesn't feel like you're going to get anywhere," Sally said, "but with community it feels like, together, people can do something."

Shifters and dropouts were somewhat less inclined than persisters to report close friendships in their peace groups and none were living in a communal arrangement with other activists. When a strong sense of community exists, especially when people are living together, commitment is reinforced and strengthened. But having good friends in a peace group does not guarantee persistence, as we see in the cases of the shifters and dropouts. Other social forces may be stronger than the activist's community ties and may consequently shift the balance of commitment and eventually lead to exit. Still, evidence from this study suggests that the more fully the activist is drawn into the community, the less chance there is of departure from the movement.

Persisters became a part of the peace community, valued the people in it, and felt the community supported them in their individual efforts. For many, maintaining that sense of community was an important goal, independent of one's efforts to make peace. David was an exception. His case shows that bonds to other parts of the movement may be strong enough to ensure persistent activism in the absence of community. Each person's commitment has its own unique pattern, characterized by some long-term commitment indicators and not others. This suggests that there are several ways a long-term commitment can be constructed. It also points up the importance of identifying the necessary conditions for maintaining commitment, one being socialization to the appropriate beliefs.

MAINTAINING THE BELIEF IN PERSONAL RESPONSIBILITY

Persisters believed strongly that they had a personal responsibility to help others, to return something to society, and to create a more peaceful world together. This was a common thread in their stories as they spoke about being in peace activism because it was the right thing to do. This sense of responsibility was an important commitment-making force, for it was an inner resolve, reinforced by other conditions.

Some persisters described this strong sense of responsibility to engage in peace and social justice work as growing from their childhood socialization; others developed it when they were older as they began to see a world in crisis. It was crisis which called upon them to act. Some persisters could no longer think about this responsibility as a choice. "There's no getting around the sense of responsibility I guess, " Grant said. "It's not something I really have a choice about. I can't ignore that without ignoring who I am."

Being responsible became a part of who persisters were, a part of their identities. To be irresponsible about activism would have made them feel guilty. This was also true for some shifters, like Beth.

> Being personally responsible gives meaning to my life. I feel very identified with the women and children who suffer the most from war, violence, and sexism. It's a personal issue. I feel I would personally benefit from the changes. And the injustices make me furious, so my activism is an outlet for that. It's a constructive outlet for my anger, and I feel bad if I don't do it, and I feel good if I do, generally. I feel crummy if I'm not doing something, crummy about myself. It is part of my ideal self to be involved, definitely a part of my value system—a good person is involved. And if I'm not involved, then I'm not living up to my ideals.

Beth's words convey the sense our respondents had about personal responsibility as an aspect of their activist identities. It was a necessity dictated by their sense of self. Their personal ethics demanded responsibility and, when they failed to be responsible, they felt "crummy." Thus, they could not imagine a life without activism, be it for peace, social justice, or environmental protection. Beth's comment also shows how activism is shaped not only by beliefs, identity, and collective incentives, but by personal, selective ones, such as the self respect one feels from being true to basic values.[3]

When persisters reached the point where they regarded their personal responsibility to work for social change as an integral part of their lives, there was little possibility they would drop out. If they did, as Beth's case shows, they would shift to another cause rather than quitting activism entirely. They might withdraw for a time to recover their energies, but it was unlikely that they would withdraw permanently. For them, social activism was so central to their lives that they no longer questioned their involvement in it. "To me personal responsibility feels like it's just a part of life," Jennifer said. "I mean, it's sort of like brushing your teeth. It's just something you do." Many persisters came to share this view as they integrated their core identities as peace activists into their daily lives. This integration reinforced their commitment. Shifters and dropouts also felt this strong sense of responsibility when they were engaged in peace action. Among the shifters, Beth renewed her commitment to work against domestic violence; Suzanne turned her attention to spirituality and herbal medicine, where she is helping people heal their bodies and souls; Pauline recommitted herself to solar energy development; and Phillip became involved in the issue of population control.

Even among the dropouts, there was either a plan to return to activism at some point or peripheral involvement in peace and social justice issues. Ron developed a career as a mediator and is currently working for interpersonal and intergroup peace. Allen is a long-time political radical temporarily out of activism who will probably return when an issue captures his interest. Tina is still a war resister who keeps her income below the taxable level. Monica left activism to tend to personal matters, but plans to become involved in health issues when she has time. Helen left because of financial and family pressures in order to pursue a new career, but she remains active in a local Quaker community. Ed left activism to return to teaching, where he continues to address the issues of war and peace. So, even though the dropouts are no longer active in peace movement organizations, they have not completely abandoned their work for change.

VARIATION OF COMMITMENT INTENSITY

An activist's commitment ebbs and flows. Its strength varies as a result of changing circumstances on the national or world scene, the amount of personal time and energy available, and the pressures of everyday life. There are specific social forces which affect the strength of a person's commitment to the movement.

Forces Leading to a Decline of Commitment

Persisters mentioned several factors which decreased the strength of their commitment. David emphasized major political disasters, such as failing to stop the U.S. from going to war in the Persian Gulf and the reelection of Ronald Reagan. While those events made him despair, they were not reason enough for him to leave the movement. "What makes people quit," he told us, "is the in-fighting because that's day in and day out, and it just wears you down."

Others felt that their commitment declined because of such factors as Congressional approval of the MX missile, competing family or career responsibilities, or the physical and emotional exhaustion of a protracted struggle with militarism. Matt reached this point during the Gulf War.

> I was working day and night to stem the flow of blood before it happened, just working myself into the ground. This gradually lowered my resistance to negative thinking. I became pretty despairing about all of it, and burned out. That was a time when I needed to take a break. It was not to question my commitment but only to restore myself and get back into it. But that situation weakened my ability to go on.

Many persisters mentioned the period immediately after a major action as a time when their commitment declined. A crisis of the magnitude of the Gulf War calls for enormous amounts of time and energy. Physical and emotional exhaustion can occur after weeks of meetings and demonstrations, then profound disappointment can set in because all that effort produced no results. While trying circumstances such as these are not likely to destroy the commitment of persisters, they can lead to a temporary decline in commitment intensity. During this time, it is not uncommon for persisters to retreat temporarily to recover their energies, their inspiration, and their will to go on.

Forces Leading to an Increase of Commitment

Persisters reported an increase in the strength of their commitment when a major crisis, such as a war or nuclear testing, was occurring. For example, Jennifer reported a dramatic increase in the time she spent organizing actions and writing letters during the Contra War in Nicaragua. The Gulf War had the same effect on her. This escalation of commitment was typical for persisters, shifters and dropouts, especially during the first weeks of a crisis event. A crisis of the magnitude of the Gulf War ignited their interest, so they were even more willing than usual to organize their lives for peace activism.

Being arrested also demanded more of these activists, which, in turn, increased their commitment. Diane remembered a protest at Lowry Air Force Base which required that kind of dedication. "I was arrested three times with a group of protesters and after the third time we ended up in court. It took a lot of energy and time to plan how to go through that trial together."

While crises and actions were mentioned most often as increasing the strength of a commitment, small victories also elevated peoples' commitment, as did seeing everyone pulling together on a project, enthusiastic people joining the cause, and many acting at considerable personal cost. Then, there was the influence of the peace community and the quality of the people in it. Just being around supportive people tended to elevate commitment, according to Susan. "There may be times when you're slumping real bad," she told us, "but you keep coming in because of the kind of people you're working with. They keep encouraging me and I keep learning from them."

CONCLUSION

Most persisters felt bonded to the important sectors of the movement—to the peace group's ideology, judging its beliefs to be compatible with their own; to the organization, thinking it was functioning effectively and in appropriate ways; to leadership, concluding that leaders were doing a good job and were acting in the spirit of the group's principles; and to the community, feeling they had close friends in the group and belonged there. These bonds are shown in Figure 4.1.

David's case was interesting because it revealed how an activist can form bonds to some sectors of a peace organization but not others. He was bonded to his organization's ideology and its structure, but had a relatively weak bond to the community. Because of the group's egalitarian structure, there was no discernible leadership toward which to feel loyal.

His case shows the importance of peace-oriented beliefs in preserving commitment; that an individual's inner convictions can be strong enough to overcome weaker bonds to some aspects of the movement organization and the community. The structure of David's commitment illustrates the point that there are different ways a peace commitment can be constructed to produce persistence.

Figure 4.1: Commitment Growth and Fluctuation

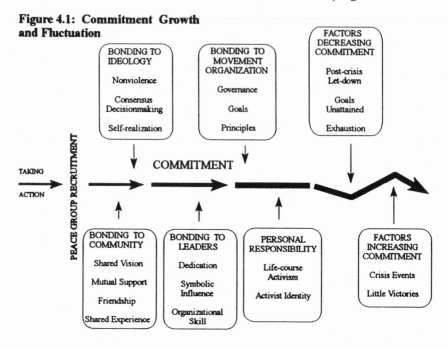

When a bond had been formed, then broken, as we saw with Beth and Monica, disillusionment with the group might follow. This supports the notion that these bonds are important for preserving commitment. How many and how strong they must be to sustain an individual's commitment is contingent on the strength of beliefs and the extent to which an activist identity has been formed. When these internal conditions exist, the outer bonds may not have to be as strong. When both are strong, a sustained commitment is almost insured. This explains, in large measure, why most persisters could maintain their peace and social justice commitment for long periods of time in the face of many disappointments.

Beliefs are one of the most important influences on commitment. Our career peace activists kept doing the work because they held strong beliefs about the kind of world they wanted to create; about themselves as people called upon to help others;

about their responsibility for solving the problems of violence and poverty; and about the importance of living their beliefs as a central aspect of their personal integrity, even when results fell short of their goals. While there were bonds to their movement organizations which encouraged commitment, their beliefs made peace and social justice work important for them regardless of its impact. These beliefs were part of their identity and peace action was an integral part of their lives.

NOTES

1. Howard S. Becker, "Notes on the Concept of Commitment," *American Journal of Sociology*, 66 (1960), pp. 32-40.

2. There is an additional way that individuals can become bonded to a movement. We have described this bond elsewhere as arising from social ritual. See "Peace Movements: The Role of Commitment and Community in Sustaining Member Participation," in Spencer, *op. cit.*

3. For an interesting analysis of the interplay between selective and collective incentives in motivating participation in social movements, see Mark Lichbach, "What Makes Rational Peasants Revolutionary?" *World Politics*, 46 (1994), pp. 382-417.

5

VISION, EFFECTIVENESS, AND URGENCY

After joining a peace organization, persisters bonded to it in various ways, thereby ensuring their long-term commitment. Other influences also served to strengthen that commitment— their shared vision of social change, perceptions about move- ment effectiveness, and feelings about the urgency for peace action. These are the issues we explore in this chapter.

A COMMON VISION OF SOCIAL CHANGE

The sustained commitment of persisters was aided by a clearly articulated vision of the peaceful world toward which they were working. It was a preferred future that appeared with remark- able consistency in their stories. However, this common vision had to be matched within their peace groups by a sense of community purpose. Internal difficulties in their organizations produced stress for some. Personality conflicts, unrealistically high expectations, and the inability of the group to meet personal needs contributed to the departure of others. Rarely did this result from a conflict between their individual perspectives and the orientation of their organizations. Most often it was rooted in what some called "failures of community." Michael described this failure in one case, where a staff member left the Rocky Mountain Peace Center after being criticized by other staff for not showing a sufficiently strong commitment to the cause.

Persisters contributed to a sense of community by reaching agreement about the definition of the social problem, the method of analysis for assessing it, and a prescription for change in order to act upon that understanding. These common ways of framing peace and social justice concerns provided a common discourse within the movement and with potential allies. Snow and Benford emphasize the importance to an organization of aligning its frame of problem analysis with those of potential allies and sympathetic constituencies. They note, for example, that in the 1980s, because the nuclear "freeze initiative framed the problem in a narrow and highly compartmentalized fashion, subsequent attempts to encompass other peace issues and link them to the nuclear threat were exceedingly difficult."[1]

The peace visions of the groups with which our activists worked were by no means identical and those organizations had different issue priorities. One would expect that activists at the Rocky Mountain Peace Center, committed to radical social change and to living that vision here and now, might conceive a peace future somewhat differently than SANE FREEZE activists who were interested primarily in dismantling the military-industrial complex. Yet, there was substantial alignment of the frames of analysis of these two groups, reflecting a good deal of agreement about what they were working toward.

The Threat and the Peace Vision

Our study was conducted during a period of historical transition. The images of threat motivating our activists were not as clear as they might have been during the Cold War, when nuclear holocaust seemed a real possibility. Yet, war was still "Enemy Number One" for them, since the U.S. had recently emerged from war in the Persian Gulf. War-making remained for them a systemic threat in the form of a single, unchecked superpower, with its military institutions seeking new justifications for maintaining their Congressional appropriations. David was alarmed by what he saw as a continuing search for new roles for the armed forces aimed at preserving U.S. military hegemony around the globe. "We have this huge military and, if it is at the service of Japan and the European Community, it will develop such vast power it cannot be rivaled."

Our activists' peace vision was an inclusive one that went beyond demilitarization. It assumed, as Sally put it, "that peace also necessitates justice in society and that whites can be allies for people of color who have suffered most from structural inequality." Martha described peace in similar terms as "having the world work more efficiently for everybody." Nancy voiced a broader conception of peace, shared by most of the people in our study, that the movement was now freed from the nuclear threat to focus more on the "domestic issues" that inhibited peace.

Our persisters' vision was also a progressive one, of a peace process building over decades and centuries, the result of innumerable individual efforts, that by themselves could be perceived as no more than negligible attacks on social and political violence. June saw it as an "accumulation of all these little bits of activity that are going on that plant the seeds for all of us to look differently at issues or begin to question or wonder about them." From memory and in great detail, Ruth traced the contributions of a single peace organization, the Women's International League for Peace and Freedom (WILPF), over nearly a century.

This view of peace development, as a process stretching far into the past, reflects the shared assumption of our persisters that peace is slow to develop and those who would build it must be prepared for long term commitment. Nancy's involvement reflected that indeterminate time dimension as she spoke about the persistence of racial injustice.

> One of the problems we face in this country is that people are accustomed to the quick fix, and there are no quick fixes in issues of race. The problem took 250 years to develop, so I don't see a quick fix. I'm in it for what I consider a long term.

Without this long-term view of development, peace activism can be difficult for movement members as they go from problem to problem and war to war, especially in a society that so celebrates winning. "This is a business where you lose a lot of times," Jack told us, "and that's frustrating to people. I don't think it's easy to hang in there. And if people don't have a peer group that is supportive in other ways, it's difficult."

Living the Vision

Earlier, we saw how many persisters designed their personal lives to better witness for their peace vision. "Witness" was a powerful concept among persisters. "To fight for peace is such a funny expression when you think of it," Lynn said. "I'd much more embrace the notion of witness. We witness peace and maybe even we are peace and that has a real influence."

Moving away from the conception of peace as a condition toward peace as a "way of life" is difficult to accomplish. June said that it is not "stopping the production of this or that weapon, or success with a particular piece of legislation you were working for. You're just going to live it. No wrapped package for you, ever."

If living peace is difficult for the individual persister, it is an almost superhuman task at the organizational level, even in movement organizations for which it is a primary goal. It places an additional burden of responsibility on the organization and requires an added measure of energy and patience. Peace organizations operate with the same developmental stages, group dynamics, and structural constraints as movement organizations generally. In organizations which are consciously being faithful to consultation, consensus, and the nonviolent interaction of their members, the strain produced by the gap between ideal and real may be too much for some members. Beth identified "group dysfunction" as the reason she left peace action for the women's movement. "Sustaining cohesion," she felt, was a special problem for her group.

The peace organizations most serious about "living peace" expend much time and energy trying to resolve conflicts that any organization would experience. The Rocky Mountain Peace Center, according to Michael, was not "immune" from such conflict. "We've had our share of it and we're working very hard to develop a better way to resolve it." It is often a draining effort as "all the individuals in the group bring their baggage and it's really hard to sort it out. We get into such intense things, almost like a therapy session, where we go into a person's life."

According to Grant, peace activists who thought they were "part of something different from the rest of the world," discover that "the same human faults and frailties, everything that is true of human beings as people, who can be selfish and greedy and all the rest, can also be true in a peace organization." This realization can be disillusioning. Carden emphasizes the importance of working for what one believes as an incentive for activists.[2] There is apparently a powerful psychological pay-off for those who commit themselves to bringing society closer to what it "should be." For peace activists, then, the conditions of "non-peace" among themselves may be particularly disturbing. How can they create peace in the world without first achieving it within their own organizations?

The dissonance between the preferred and the actual is a continuing problem for the organizations in which our persisters work. Inordinate amounts of time and energy are expended to eliminate it. They may be unclear about the proper distribution of their group's resources between maintaining peace within their organizations and their external movement goals. One is giving "so much attention and energy to the organization that you're missing the cause" is how Rebecca put it.

These organizations are often paralyzed by what might be called "tyrannical democracy." They attract people accustomed to expressing themselves in public. Since consensus decision-making is highly valued, Brian told us, "the process takes over." Hours can be spent on a trivial issue.

When Vision Fails

Despite the great care our activists took building a coherent vision of peace for the world and their organizations, some left the movement because coherence was not achieved. Some found it too stressful trying to live a vision outside the societal mainstream. Ron, who has ceased to be active, put it bluntly.

> It's very difficult to be a peace activist, especially in this war-oriented society where dedication to a principle is ridiculed and is discriminated against in a number of ways. It is very difficult for activists to follow through because their perceptions of what's wrong expose elemental contradictions in society, contradictions others just don't want to see.

Some activists learn after a time that they are a "bad fit" with an organization. This may involve a divergence of visions, a distancing of their frame of reference from that of their group. Rebecca felt that one movement colleague who had fallen away "found the organization going a different way and didn't have the energy to make the shift."

Differing commitment levels in an organization may be a source of friction that causes someone to leave. Those with more time, energy, or ideological zeal to contribute may be quite intolerant of others. One respondent who left an organization criticized a "holier than thou feeling about the place" that discounted less than total commitment to nonviolence.

An activist who left one peace organization often took up work in another. These people have "grounded commitment" Jack said, "staying power." Then there were people who joined for a limited period, recruited for a specific skill they had, such as knowing Russian. Their commitment was necessarily different from that of the core membership and they were less likely to stay committed.

Finally, activists persist in response to how well their organization meets their personal needs. They are drawn to it in part for the promise it holds as a vehicle for their commitment. If they subsequently do not find acceptance, validation, and productive engagement there, they may leave.

Peace groups appear to have a special problem engaging short-term volunteers with meaningful work. They need such people but they often use them poorly and misunderstand their needs. Rebecca spoke of her organization's incapacity "to help people do what they want to do or integrate them into the plan and modify it so that they're part of it." Many of these volunteers have the potential for long-term commitment. Others are simply seeking ways to work out their anger at the "system." That emotion can block useful exchange with the persisters in the group. "Many of them come with so much anger," Rebecca recalled, "that they really don't have anything to say for a long time and there is no way to heal them so they can move past that." The involvement of such people in effective peace action is often left to chance.

The inability of an organization to usefully engage its workers in realizing its peace vision frustrates persisters. While they have the commitment and patience to stick with it, rank-and-file volunteers generally do not. Still, those with high commitment and long experience can also find their group's weaknesses intolerable, as Beth did. She left, a co-worker told us, when she felt "her ideas were not being heard, especially her concern that to be efficient and effective the Peace Center needed to be more structured. She'd been saying this in meetings over and over and they never heard it." She also felt that her concern about the "inherent sexism" in peace movement organizations was not seriously addressed, a criticism she regarded as widely shared among women who left the movement.

One of the personal needs peace organizations cannot normally meet for their members is for immediate gratification on the peace front. They may not successfully communicate to their recruits the need for a long-term perspective. This is a problem Sally discussed.

> Some people get overwhelmed and discouraged when they hear what the real issues are. They think that you can solve a problem in a month. They have no realistic understanding of what the forces are out there. They have a real short attention span for dealing with things.

Even when a peace organization has a compelling and coherent vision, a sense of community, and is satisfying many needs for activists, stubborn problems will remain. Persisters' efforts may be constrained by their racial, national or gender status, an obstacle no level of commitment to activism can overcome. Nancy spoke of a program of apartheid education that had failed in a black community "because the person who went to that community was not black. I probably felt the most frustration when the staff just didn't seem to understand how important that was." There will be situations like this where vision, role, personal attributes, and the peace action setting simply cannot come together successfully.

There will also be failures to create the full sense of community necessary for bonding the activist to others. Even when that develops, some, who have the potential to become persistent activists, may hold back simply because they are personally incapable of connecting with others and prefer to be "loners."

PERCEIVED EFFECTIVENESS

Our activists' perception of effectiveness in their organizations and the positive impact of the movement as a whole was an important contributor to their persistence. Because their vision of a peaceful society was so different from what existed, they felt that desired change would come only in small increments. Yet, even if they perceived little or no success, they felt the obligation to continue simply because peace and social justice work was the right thing to do. Staying with peace action, knowing its results would be slow and incremental, was possible partly because they felt accepted in their peace organizations and could comfortably perform their activist role there.

Location in an organization that valued them and had a vision matching their own was important for enabling them to persist.

So, too, was their sense of personal accomplishment and their feeling that the peace movement was making progress. Since most of our persisters saw peace development as occurring over the long term, their claims of success in any particular action against violence were generally modest ones.

Their definition of "success" was as multidimensional as their peace commitments. They might be simultaneously committed to building an organization, persuading the U.S. Congress to vote against military intervention somewhere in the world, and raising their children according to the principles of nonviolence. They might feel somewhat successful in all, some, or none of these efforts. Even if they saw no positive impact from their peace action anywhere, they could still be satisfied with having worked to implement their values. In asking themselves, "Did my work make a difference?" they could always answer that it did for them. So, our persistent activists had several ways of judging the success of their work.

Levels of Impact

As one might expect, the more remote the target of change from the locus of peace action, the weaker were our activists' claims of positive impact. Their judgments of substantial influence were uniformly clear and emphatic when it came to projects at the local level. Arlene, a leader in the Boulder-Dushanbe Sister Cities project, spoke of the "remarkable" and "important" effects the work had in changing public attitudes in the two communities. Jennifer, active in a Central American city-twinning program, voiced a good deal of satisfaction with what had been accomplished there. She felt it was easier to measure impact in such "specific" and "direct" types of peace action. Face-to-face interaction and exchange visits provided direct feedback about the influence peace action was having.

Peace action against local military installations such as the Rocky Flats nuclear weapons plant was also judged by persisters to have been influential in bringing about change. In this case, however, activists were less willing to claim a direct cause-and-effect impact of their work, simply because of the complexity of the nuclear weapons decision-making process. Their targets of change had been officials and workers at several levels: At the plant itself; in Denver, Washington, and Moscow; and in the

Soviet weapons-producing communities. Don felt that his group's involvement with the national Nuclear Weapons Facilities Task Force network "had some slight impact probably on the national debate and discussion."

Ron saw his organization's impact as particularly significant in permitting movement members to "think globally and act locally," and to live "the personal as political." He found it "clearly a force in the community during the Gulf War when a lot of people who are less active needed something to turn to." He thought it had a "major impact on the eventual shutdown of Rocky Flats and on nuclear testing."

Activists' perceptions of success in their work beyond the local community could be positive with respect to particular actions and less certain in terms of the impact on the larger problems of violence and social injustice. Diane, for instance, felt her group's work in getting Western Airlines to cease transporting political refugees back to El Salvador was extremely influential. With respect to the larger problem, however, it was "hard to say how we have had any impact, but we can claim to be part of the movement that's helped to bring about the end of the war in El Salvador. That's a significant change."

Redefining Success

Given their view of peace-building as a long-term process, persisters rarely defined success simply in terms of tasks accomplished. Rebecca saw great merit in the intergenerational character of her group's work, bringing together as it did volunteers of all ages in nonviolent direct action. She spoke of the success of the Nevada Test Site Action as providing a measure of community "maturation" and as building a lasting peace network in the area. Michael felt great satisfaction in the evolution of "a kind of infrastructure of peace, social justice, and environmental organizations that has been established in the country." When our activists saw such a "peace system" emerging within the decade when they were so active, they quite naturally experienced a sense of accomplishment.

For Jack, whose work has been through a long-standing Quaker peace organization, "germination" and "spinoff" of new groups from the established ones was an important dynamic and an indicator of peace movement development. His satisfaction was derived largely from seeing those organizational seedlings take root and flourish.

Success was sometimes defined by our persisters not as movement forward but as ground not lost. Satisfaction could be found in successful "holding actions," as Susan said.

> It seems like we're on the losing side of things so many times. The situation is really bad now and it sounds like we're not moving ahead at all, but how much further back would we be if there weren't groups like this at all? One of the things that keeps me going is thinking about it in those terms.

Brian described it as "kind of putting your finger in the dike rather than actually moving forward." And Matt remembered his group's action during the Gulf War as "a candle in the wind, a flickering light in a place of darkness." Such perceptions reflected a feeling among persisters that peace action would always be an activity of a small minority and it would produce results slowly. Only on rare occasions would they find themselves swimming with the current. This is why, for persisters, being ethically anchored was more important and satisfying than being successful.

Persistent activists had yet another way of viewing success. They judged their peace action from the perspective of process more than results. June felt that peace "isn't something you get done, it's something you do more than anything else. So it makes it more reasonable when certain things you wanted to see happen didn't get done quite as you expected and in the time you expected." Lynn agreed that persisters "do what we do because it's what we stand on, what we believe and we don't measure the consequences."

Despite persisters' reluctance to judge their work by the usual productivity standard, tangible success at some level was important for maintaining their commitment. Some derived satisfaction from the act of creating a method or organization, independent of results. Others emphasized the importance and value of small successes, little victories that can have a cumulative effect over time. One cannot know, June reasoned, the "ramifications of the work on a broader level through a ripple effect." Susan spoke of persisters who stuck with peace action as "great souls taking little steps." Or, as Ed put it: "We're kind of like foot soldiers out in the battle. No single infantryman wins the battle, but ten divisions together probably do."

Not only do small victories make a difference, but small changes can have an effect, as we discover in Helen's account of her attempt to convince Soviet officials to participate in her sister cities project.

> They thought the whole idea of sister cities was CIA. I could tell they were really not interested. The guy was leafing through the papers. I had thrown in everything including an article about a balalaika band in Boulder, the only paper this man was interested in. He said, "there's a balalaika band in Boulder?" I didn't know a lot about it but had to talk about it anyway. They had said that they wouldn't dream of talking with a city of less than 100,000. It was after that, in their next release on sister cities, that the form had been changed. In parentheses it said "or maybe 80,000."

Persisters expressed a constant optimism about their work even though they could not really measure its success. Activists without that positive view of the glass half-full rather than half-empty tended not to stay. Diane described one who "did an awful lot of reading about things, and decided that nothing she did would make a difference" and left the movement. In contrast, persisters possessed "grounded optimism." Their assessment of accomplishments seemed to ring true and their thinking reflected realism as they referred to failures and successes, of "dramatic victories few and very far between," or of "making a lot of progress we aren't even aware of."

Perhaps the most powerful positive feedback persisters received from their peace work was their sense of judgment vindicated, of taking the morally right path. Grant expressed this clearly.

> I was part of the first group in Colorado ever to successfully utilize the lesser of evils defense in a political protest court case. It was very satisfying to know that I had been involved in a process where, in a public and nonviolent way, we stood up for what we believed was right and were upheld by the court.

Those Who Left

Most of our respondents who left the movement were not dissatisfied with the impact of their peace groups but left for other reasons. Allen, for instance, felt that his was one of a "few core organizations that hang in there and go through the dry times and just keep punching out the educational programs, parades, and visuals." Suzanne expressed frustration not with her organization but with the movement and the "uphill struggle," but also was hopeful and excited at its accelerated pace in more recent years. But problems within their organizations were a cause of departure for some. Beth felt "quite satisfied" with the work her group had done, yet "had a lot of frustrations with the group and would have done things differently. We could have been more effective. It's a real mix of feelings." Only one of those who dropped out of activism expressed dissatisfaction with her organization and its impact. Monica was particularly bothered with power plays by the group's director and what she perceived as pervasive religiosity and pacifism that changed its ecumenical character.

Several who left peace activism were troubled, however, by the uncertainty of the work's impact. Pauline said that "one of the tough things in public activism is that, with the most interesting projects, you're least sure of what your impact has been." Allen was convinced that the impact had been "not enough, not nearly enough. Little victories are great but it's got to be more than taking a few bows and having a few people notice. We're not effective enough until the system changes."

PERCEIVED URGENCY FOR PEACE ACTION

Persisters expressed a strong sense of urgency about peace development, a perception which helped preserve their commitments. They felt compelled to continue the work because of the vision of peace they held and because they feared the negative consequences if peace was absent. This sense of urgency was directly related to political events. With the end of the Cold War and the consequent disappearance of the threat of nuclear annihilation, vision replaced threat as their primary motivation.

Persistent activists viewed their work as unending. In other words, peace action was not a task that was accomplished, but an endless working toward social change. Persisters commonly identified three needs to which they were responding—their own personal need to continue, a need within their own society for the work they do, and global emergency.

Personal Need

Some activists were quite clear about the personal gain they experienced from their persistence. Rebecca described the process as "self-generation. I find it almost depressing to not be doing something aimed at the big picture because the way we live now does not work for anybody." Ruth felt her peace activism was essential for her mental and physical health. "I do it because it's really what I believe in, it's part of living the kind of life I want to lead. If I give up on peace work, I'm in big trouble, depressed, too sick to breathe or something like that." Others expressed the need for a continuing connection with like-minded people, or for an outlet for their anger at the war system and social injustice.

Yet, for some, commitment existed in tandem with the need to escape from it. Susan spoke of feeling "so compelled that if I stopped being active I couldn't function. And sometimes I wish I didn't feel that way, so I could stop. Yes, sometimes I feel like I just want to leave it all." When the need to escape became overwhelming, the activist did leave, sometimes for a short period of time to recover or, if really burned out, for good.

Societal and Global Need

Most of these activists spoke of the need to transform public policy through organized protests in order to prevent future wars. They voiced what is a movement-wide call for structural modifications in how nations defend themselves. [3] For persisters, the need for structural change remained constant. They did not cease working when a particular milestone was reached. In fact, the greater the momentum the movement built up in the 1980s, the more activists felt it was important to keep building on it. "The world situation has changed so dramatically," observed Michael. "It amazes me how many nonviolent movements there are and how they keep springing up."

Many of our persisters saw the larger nonviolence movement developing rapidly on the global level. They were encouraged to see the various movements for peace and social justice arising around the world. Despite their moderate optimism about the growth of these movements, they cautioned against letting up on the effort. Inertia and "business as usual" are powerful forces. Rebecca saw "a tendency to back off right now and I think that's a big mistake. The peace movement has to stay right in there," because systems which encourage war and violence, she felt, will not back off except for temporary tactical advantage.

Jennifer's frustration resulted from her inability to bring about change on a sufficiently large scale. "Dissatisfaction is rooted in the situation and the need for on-going work. This is a real mission because there's a lot still to be done." One persister saw "as many wars going on as we've ever had. And not the skills to stop them," and felt that the end of the Cold War increased political and social instability in a world more dangerous than ever in many ways.

Persisters felt that peace action was even more vital in peacetime than during wars. "Peace is more than the absence of war" is how Arlene put it. Matt characterized that broader concept of peace as including "the peace of people's lives." Specifically, he was referring to environmental hazards such as ozone depletion which produces violence in the lives of skin cancer victims and their families. The interweaving of the violence of war, environmental degradation, and poverty allowed these activists to shift the focus of their attention naturally from one issue to another because all fell within the scope of their peace vision.

Persisters hoped that peace action would at least remain constant, if not increase, in response to new threats and new possibilities on the international level. However, with the collapse of the Soviet Union and the end of the Cold War, there was no longer a rallying point for peace activists and a new approach was needed. As June said, "When you get rid of 'the enemy' as we've been led to believe existed, I think it's harder to have people come together and formulate ways of working for peace." These activists perceived the need to move beyond threat toward new peace-supportive alliances in order to take full advantage of the new potential for peace. Their discourse was studded with "unparalleled opportunities," "urgent situations," "redirected energies" and "grasping the options."

One final observation can be made about the role of perceived need in sustaining the commitment of persisters. The passing of time and increased life experience can influence the sense of urgency activists feel. Jennifer mentioned this.

> As I got a bit older, I began to see that, well, these problems were a long time in the making; they were going to be a long time in the solving. I still feel an urgency, but not the same as I did when I was

20, or when there was a very tangible danger. I think I also work unconsciously to keep a sense of urgency at bay, because I feel like a desperate place is not a place to be working from. You need to moderate your sense of immediate urgency so you're not overwhelmed, but you also need to see the urgency of the work so you can go on day to day.

Departure from the Peace Movement

Persisters maintained a measured sense of urgency and need as they carried on their peace efforts. They did so from a vision that will be long in coming to realization, by replacing threat with opportunity in their assessment of need, and by permitting life experience to temper their expectations and time horizons. They would not agree with one dropout's assessment that "our goals had been achieved, it was now time to do something else."

Those who left the movement sometimes did so because they perceived that the threat they were working against had disappeared. Pauline felt "that the real emergency was, if not over, so diminished that I could go back to solar energy issues where I really knew what I was talking about." Phillip shifted his commitment to population and habitat destruction issues "once the tension started to drop and the risk of destruction seemed to lessen." Helen, who had worked for U.S.-Soviet understanding through city-twinning, had a feeling of closure when the question "'But what about the Russians?' had become irrelevant. So in a sense, the raison d'etre for that work was gone." The perception of the need to continue what they had been doing changed dramatically for these people and, with a decline in the urgency of peace issues in their thinking came a growing interest in other social problems or responsibilities.

As noted earlier, personal needs are a primary reason for departure from the peace movement. Often, the need to be elsewhere eclipses the urgency of movement issues for those who have already made sacrifices, who are weary of the struggle, or who simply must respond to other pressures which were put aside as they did their movement work. "More time for themselves and their families" was frequently mentioned, as was the need to get away from it all.

We should emphasize that the departure of those who left the movement may be temporary. The suggestion was strong among them that they would be "on call" for the movement. A new international crisis, or a more belligerent or interventionist U.S. government, could bring some of them quickly back from "the reserves" into "active duty." Still, this was a group whose commitment to participate in peace action had changed at a fundamental level, a change which set them off from persisters.

SOCIAL REALITY CONSTRUCTED

Persisters appeared to be held in their commitments by a reality they constructed and shared—a reality represented in similar world views and problem definitions, and in a common discourse that gave meaning and coherence to their movement work. Gamson shows how important such a discourse was in the development of the anti-nuclear power movement. [4]

Persisters shared a common vision of a peaceful world, agreed that the obstacles to realizing that vision were violence, war, and social injustice, and embraced a notion of peace activism as total and continuing commitment to the cause. This vision was part of a shared reality continually reinforced within their movement organizations, social networks and common discourse. Together, they constructed a social reality which kept them involved. [5] While that reality was similar in some ways to that held by people who were peace activists for the short term, there was also something unique about it.

First, persisters saw themselves as distinct from the thousands of people who have been involved in peace action for short periods of time or who were willing to participate in public protests at selected times. Persisters knew that they are the ones who keep at it. As Jack said:

> We are by nature a remnant of a consistent, devoted movement. To survive and to maintain my kind of consistent commitment, I have accepted the remnant role—a belief that come hell or high water, the truth will persist, though it may not prevail.

This is part of the social reality persisters developed, of being true to their ethical principles and of living peace in their daily lives, not just working for peace and social justice in the world. This shared belief keeps them active "come hell or high water" and it integrates peace work and living, so there is no way for them to leave peace activism. They would have to quit living to do so.

It was in this context that persisters spoke of peace more often as a way of life than as a movement. "It's not a movement in any one shape or form, but that part of humanity that holds true to the laws of love, openness, and friendliness," said Jack. Peace action was hard for Grant to conceive of as a movement. "I guess I don't really recognize that there is such a thing as the movement. There are communities of people wrestling with questions of what it means to live with integrity, to live out of our values. That's the work that really needs to be done." This life-integrating function of their peace activism may well be the most important factor contributing to the maintenance of their commitment. It gives meaning to their lives, as they do something that really matters to them. Arlene expressed this very well. "Personally, I'm doing what I want to do. I feel I'm making a difference. For me that's a very important part of my life."

Another dimension of the social reality persisters shared was the conviction that violence, not war, is at the center of destructive conflict in the world. Seeing so much violence in the world engaged their idealism and affected their feeling about the urgency of peace action. "Peace efforts are probably just as urgent as they ever were," Brian explained. "Even if the end of the Cold War may have lessened the nuclear threat, it certainly hasn't lessened violence in the world."

Although the idealism of persisters heavily colored their social reality, there was a good deal of realism there as well. Their view of the magnitude of the problem, of their own resources, and of the strength of their opponents rang true. For example, Brian was quite surprised at what the movement had accomplished "given the limited numbers we had and the kinds of organizations and money that we're up against." There was also a fair amount of realism in their willingness to criticize themselves and the movement. Susan thought that "the peace movement itself sometimes can be really selfish. It takes so long to make a decision because everybody seems to want their own way. A lot of times, peace activists don't bend very much." Another criticism was that the peace movement lacked flexibility and cultural diversity. Nancy's "biggest complaint about the peace movement has been that it's been very white and middle class. Ownership of the movement has been hard to give up, inclusion of other groups has been hard for people in leadership positions."

Thus, peace persisters operate in a social reality in which they know they are a minority who cannot "put down the torch."

They integrate peace action into their lives and do so because they are guided by strong ethical values which make taking action their personal responsibility. They are realistic and practical in the way they see the political situation they have to work within. They look for the weaknesses in themselves and the movement so they can change them for better results. In some ways, there is a sense of the artist here, confronting the canvas day after day, struggling to capture an image because it is what one needs to do, because there is no other way to be. For persisters, peace activism has this quality.

CONCLUSION

As shown in Figure 5.1, persisters held a common vision and shared similar ideas about social reality.

There was a strong indication of a common discourse between them. They saw modest, incremental progress toward a distant goal of peace and they argued for patience in reaching it. They placed emphasis on violence as the ultimate target of change, not just its particular manifestations, such as war. They shared a socially constructed reality which, in its design, enabled and encouraged steady, measured, deliberate action over long periods.

Figure 5.1: The Shared Reality
of Persistent Activists

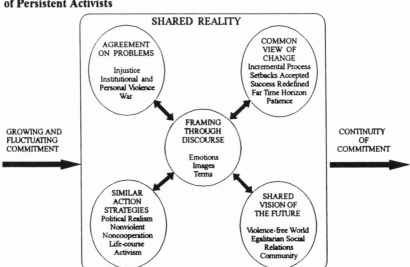

NOTES

1. David Snow and Robert Benford, "Ideology, Frame Resonance and Participant Mobilization," in Klandermans, Kriesi and Tarrow, *op. cit.*, p. 212.

2. Maren Carden, "The Proliferation of a Social Movement: Ideology and Individual Incentives in the Contemporary Feminist Movement," in Louis Kriesberg, ed., *Research in Social Movements, Conflict and Change: Volume 1* (Greenwich, CT: JAI Press, 1978), pp. 179-196.

3. A cogent analysis of the problem of linking movement success to permanent policy alteration is Pam Solo's *From Protest to Policy: Beyond the Freeze to Common Security* (Cambridge, MA: Ballinger Press, 1988).

4. William Gamson, "Political Discourse and Collective Action," in Klandermans, Kriesi and Tarrow, *op. cit.*, pp. 219-244.

5. Peter Berger and Thomas Luckman, *The Social Construction of Reality, op. cit.*

6

SOCIAL SUPPORT
AND CROSS PRESSURES

Persisters maintained their commitments partly because they patiently charted a course they knew could only be successfully navigated over the long term. They recognized that peace activism, though seldom dramatic, does produce positive results. They believed peace action was urgent and they immersed themselves in a view of social reality which sustained their activism. These were important dimensions of their commitment, but they do not fully explain it. Commitment to a movement is also affected by a larger set of social supports and cross pressures which may originate in the family, among friends, and from educational and career obligations. How these social forces affect sustained commitment is the theme of this chapter.

HOW PEACE COMMITMENTS ARE SUPPORTED

Persisters, shifters, and dropouts all reported generally strong social support for their peace and social justice commitments. It came from other activists and from people outside the peace movement.

Support from Within the Peace Community

Since close friendships were often developed with other peace activists, natural support groups formed. Activist friends were available to console and encourage when someone became discouraged, physically and emotionally exhausted, or just weary of the struggle. When an activist wanted to undertake a new project or action, those friends gave advice and support.

These support groups were so essential for carrying on movement work that many activists consciously developed them. For example, Michael was part of a group of activists which had been meeting weekly since 1984. Its focus was contemplation and social justice, where half the meeting was devoted to silence and half to discussion of change and strategy. This group backed Michael by helping him evaluate actions he was taking and by encouraging his peace efforts. This small community was one of three he was involved with, each meeting an essential need for intellectual stimulation and dialogue, for contemplation, and for planning joint actions. Although he thought these needs might have been better served within one large community of support, being involved in three smaller groups worked well for him.

Most of these activists were integrated into a support group of some kind. Grant and Lynn were living on a day-to-day basis in peace communities, although communal living arrangements were rare among our respondents. Most relied on support from activist friends or co-workers within their movement organizations, who lived in different parts of the city, but who did movement work together, played together, became angry together, and sometimes cried together. This connected them to others, which served to keep them going, even through tough times. "It's just the bonding," said Ruth, "the kind of stuff that keeps you going because you have a community of support around you wherever you go."

Support could be counted on and it was usually given unconditionally. This gave our activists a feeling of solidarity with others, of never being alone. Speaking of the group which had been supporting him and his wife in their activism for years, Jack said, with gratitude and affection: "It's a real supportive group and if something comes up, they're with us." With confidence that there were people ready to help at a moment's notice, persisters like Jack could feel more certain about initiating and engaging in peace action, even when the threat of arrest was high. They knew there was someone to back them up, someone who cared about them as part of a community of kindred spirits who shared their peace and social justice vision.

Being socially bonded is one of the most important aspects of persistent activism, feeling solidarity with others who are also sacrificing for the cause and need support. As activists help each other year after year, mutual admiration and affection develop which serve to encourage the fundamental ideas of caring, service, sacrifice, and perseverance. This fellowship anchors the activist's commitment within a larger network of community effort. Thus, while commitment is individually constructed and maintained, its durability is enhanced because it is located in community, where alliances with other activists reinforce it. Most persisters were linked to others in this way. They had activist friends whom they could count on to encourage their efforts, comfort them when conditions were tough, and help with their projects when the need arose. Only one persister, David, seemed to be at the edge of the community. He described having connections with other peace activists, but then concluded: "I don't personally feel much support there."

Without much social support, David's tenacity as a peace activist is all the more impressive, which shows how crucial inner conviction can be. His experience runs counter to the expectation that solid backing from other activists is essential for carrying on long-term peace action. Apparently, the depth of conviction that arises from strongly held peace-oriented beliefs can keep an activist involved even when minimal support is being received from others in the peace community.

Support from Outside the Peace Community

There are also sources of support from outside the peace movement which can make a difference. An activist's commitment may be affirmed and encouraged by others who, while not directly involved in movement work, respect the efforts of people who are. Immediate family members, distant relatives, non-movement friends and co-workers—these people can contribute to the maintenance of an activist's commitment by simply respecting and applauding it.

Family was an important source of support for many of these activists. While not all received their family's endorsement, many, like Diane, did. She was the only one in her family who was involved in peace-making efforts, yet the members of her family were important sources of support for her activism. "They've joked about making cookies for me if I went to jail."

The biological families of our activists tended to live at a considerable distance from them. Often separated by hundreds of miles, the support of these relatives, while important, carried less weight than the encouragement they received from spouses, children, or friends with whom they interacted on a daily basis. And, when relatives expressed negative opinions about their peace activity, they could more easily discount them, knowing they would have only limited contact with those critics.

For those heavily involved in peace activism, support from their immediate families is what counted. Most were fortunate to have spouses (or "significant others") and children who often enthusiastically endorsed their peace work. That support made a difference. Before she shifted back to solar energy activism, Pauline's husband and daughter were important supporters of her peace efforts. "You can't do this work without a supportive family," she said, "because the work cuts into your time and energy for them and they live through all this with you, including the disappointments."

Friends were another important source of support. Our activists described friends outside of the movement as key defenders of their peace efforts. Being surrounded by friends who applauded their work was hardly accidental, however, for they tended to select as friends people who reflected their own beliefs. Don mentioned this tendency as part of what he called the "self-selecting" basis of his social support, of choosing friends who shared his peace vision and his commitment to social action. As he put it: "I would find it hard to have a close relationship with a Reaganite." Beth also constructed friendships along ideological lines.

> It would be very hard for me to be an activist without moving and living in a community of people who were supporting my values. I don't like being around people very long who don't. That's very isolating and difficult to do.

Speaking of how she would choose a husband, Monica revealed her preference for an ideologically compatible mate: "If I'm ever going to be with somebody for the long haul, it's going to have to be somebody who's not in conflict with this kind of work. In fact, it's going to be a crucial factor in whom I decide to marry."

By choosing friends who shared their beliefs, persisters like Don, shifters like Beth, and dropouts like Monica developed communities of support. By avoiding people who were ideologically incompatible, they insulated themselves from a source of possible opposition. Overall, tighter bonds with like-minded others and less interaction with those who might criticize served to strengthen their commitment.

Generally, support from immediate family members, non-activist friends, and distant relatives was positive for persisters, shifters, and dropouts alike. Most felt that the encouragement they received from those outside the movement helped them carry on their movement obligations. "I think support has a substantial impact," Don noted, "that my wife and friends are supportive of my peace work, that provides encouragement and validation for what I'm doing." These networks of affirmation were a source of encouragement, a place where frustrations could be aired, disappointments worked through, and small victories celebrated. However, some activists also had people in their lives who opposed their work.

FORCES OPPOSING PEACE COMMITMENTS

Commitments exist in the tension between forces supporting and opposing them. While most of our activists reported a high level of support for their work, some did experience opposition, usually from relatives living elsewhere. Michael spoke of resistance from two sisters in another state, both Christian fundamentalists, who supported the Gulf War. But, he resisted their political leanings: "I never made the decision to cut myself off completely from my family, but I certainly made the decision that what they thought was right was not going to determine my way of seeing things." Geographical distance made opposition less influential.

Opposition from relatives was also deflected by the perception that political differences within the family were expected and respected. It was this "live and let live" philosophy about which Jack spoke.

> Some of my relatives ended up being more conservative, so we don't have close friendships, although we show up at the family reunion. We enjoy each other's company and just steer clear of what we don't have in common. At times, I'll make a statement and someone will say: "Well, I can't agree with that." After arguing about it, we'd end up saying, "Well, we ought to be sure of our positions" and "we have a right to go our separate ways."

The power of conviction also helped preserve the commitments of these activists, for they believed so strongly in the value of their movement work that even the harshest criticisms from others could not shake it. "As my conviction grew that I should be doing peace work," Don said, "I felt I'd do it regardless of what some of my colleagues felt."

Strength of belief made a difference. It prevented people from caving in to opposition. For example, June recalled being visited by a cousin who, at dinner one evening, became angry when he learned that she was involved in peace activities. While she was startled by his outburst, his hostility did not shake her position for, as she said: "I really do believe in what I do." June's conviction was shared by other activists and was probably the chief reason that opposition had little impact on their commitment. Firm in their beliefs and surrounded by people who supported them, they did not let criticism undermine their peace efforts.

Others could fend off verbal assaults on their peace work because they understood that, given the nature of peace activism, opposition had to be expected. As Susan said:

> Opposition doesn't affect my commitment as far as making me draw back because I know before I do something that I'm going to get criticized for doing it. There's a lot of people who don't agree with us and who feel strongly about that and so they're going to criticize us. I know that.

Still others, sure of their beliefs and firm in their commitment, learned to ignore opposition or, when that was impossible, to be playful in the way they dealt with it. "The way I've handled opposition is by ignoring it," said Brian. "We just don't talk about it a lot. When we do, we joke about it." When his parents were considering a visit at a time when Brian, his wife, and others were planning a demonstration, his wife told his father over the phone: "If you'd like, you can come and get tear gassed with us when you're out here that weekend. He said, 'no thanks, we'll pass on that'."

Other strategies were developed to deal with critics. Beth, a shifter, created a simple one.

> I avoid those people. I think it's important to know what their opinions are in order to understand that way of thinking, so I read about the ideas of people I don't agree with. But, I don't generally like to talk to them. During the Gulf War, I didn't want to be around anybody that didn't agree with me about the war because I was so upset about it.

Avoiding those who opposed their peace efforts helped these activists maintain their commitments.

As long as there was strong support from significant others in their lives, they could feel good about their movement work. When those close to them were less supportive, it could negatively affect their commitment, although that was rare. Jennifer explained this effect in her most recent long-term relationship, where "the guy wasn't really supportive. He didn't oppose the work, but he wasn't all that interested in it, so I felt that I went to fewer meetings, so I could spend more time with him."

It was rare for persisters, shifters, or dropouts to be in relationships where support was weak and even rarer for them to meet resistance from those with whom they lived. The normal pattern was strong endorsement for their activism from significant others. When support came from people who counted, opposition from others of less significance had little impact. In fact, for some like Matt, criticism even reinforced commitment to some degree. "Opposition inspires me. It's all the more reason to go do this work."

So, criticism and opposition appeared to have little effect on the commitment of our activists. They found ways to adapt to it, by ignoring it, by staying away from potential critics, by joking about it, and by expecting and accepting it as a natural consequence of taking an activist stand. Convinced that their cause was just, they were not fazed by opposition. It was not the main problem, according to June. "Indifference is a greater weapon than opposition, I think. That's the big thing we're fighting."

We should note that neither lack of support nor opposition pushed shifters to move from peace action to other movements or dropouts to exit from activism. Like persisters, they had good support systems for their work and they found ways to handle resistance when it emerged. Thus, opposition and lack of support were not important determinants of change in their commitments.

COMPETING AND REINFORCING RESPONSIBILITIES

Our activists had responsibilities outside their peace activities to income-producing careers, families, friendships, and, sometimes, religious groups. The strength of their peace commitment was affected by the demands these other life activities made on their time and resources. Especially important was whether responsibilities outside the movement competed with or reinforced their movement work. Overall, as these activists examined their patterns of responsibility, they found that, while some of their other life demands did compete with their movement work, it was not intense competition. Many felt that other responsibilities actually reinforced their peace and justice efforts. The main exceptions to this were Monica, Ron, and Helen, whose exit from activism was partly caused by demands in other areas of their lives.

Persisters had few seriously distracting responsibilities and, when they did, they tried to balance them to preserve the possibility of peace action. June's peace commitment was enhanced, for example, because her children had reached adulthood and were no longer living at home. She worked as a substitute teacher, which also gave her more time for activism. She was careful not to overdo her activism. She made time for other activities that were enjoyable and interesting, such as tennis and book and investment clubs. "I try to do a number of different things because I think it's important to replenish yourself. You can wear yourself out with peace work. But there's no doubt that I spend most of my time doing that work."

The conflicts between Sally's life demands were minimal and her non-movement activities generally enhanced her peace action. The person she lived with was also an activist, so there was no major competition at home. She had a part-time teaching job where she was able to teach subjects related to her peace work, while still having time to participate in movement projects. She was also modestly paid as a staff member in her peace group. Overall, her responsibilities were mutually reinforcing.

Ruth was heavily involved in peace movement projects because she was retired, a widow, and her children were raised and on their own. With few competing demands in her life, her movement work became nearly all-consuming. "Now I have to struggle to say no. My house and garden get neglected, but when my grandkids are in town, they're a top priority for me."

Initially, Jack's desire to become involved in peace action and his need to practice medicine to support his wife and children were in conflict. He was forced to scale back his peace activities until his children were grown and he was able to reduce his professional obligations. At that point, he became more involved in movement work.

Arlene was unmarried, so she did not have family matters to keep her from movement work. Although she had a full-time job, her work schedule was flexible. She could go to the daytime meetings of her peace group and make up the time by working after hours at her paying job. She established priorities where movement work often came first. Instead of using her weekends to hike in the mountains or pursue other activities, she would stay home "to write that next article for the newsletter or catch up on correspondence."

Susan balanced three fairly significant responsibilities: To peace activism, a graduate degree program, and important friendships. While graduate study was very demanding, she had no doubt about her priorities, for peace activism meant a great deal to her. When the demands of her activism and graduate studies came into conflict, her school assignments were set aside.

This tendency to prioritize their activities was especially common among persisters, who saw their peace work as the most meaningful aspect of their lives. While they attempted to balance their movement demands with their other responsibilities, they were clear that activism came first. Like most persisters, Arlene and Susan made the choice to work for peace and to forego other pleasures and opportunities.

Diane lived with two other activists, so her living situation fit nicely into her peace career. She held a part-time job in a poverty program so that, too, was in harmony with her activism.

> I don't feel like anything really competes with my peace commitment. I'm trying to live in a way where I don't need a whole lot of money and so I don't have to worry about having a job that pays a lot. I'm kind of into downward mobility. So I'm trying to live some kind of integrated life I guess.

Diane's choice to live a downwardly mobile life was not unusual among persisters. Several had turned away from conventional careers, consciously taking part-time jobs so they would have more time for activism and could pay less or no taxes to support military spending.

These activists learned to balance their responsibilities. Too much time and energy devoted to peace action could burn them out, undermine their peace careers and disturb important relationships. For example, Don was married, but without children. He described how, early in his peace career, he was so busy with various projects that he neglected his wife. In time, he became aware of this problem and corrected it, which created a more balanced and healthy foundation for his activism.

While some with conflicting demands on them engaged in a balancing act to preserve their activism, others were fortunate to have responsibilities which dovetailed. Brian's came together in this way.

> My work allows me a certain amount of flexibility and I'm not career oriented. I'm not in an organization where doing the work I do might put me in jeopardy in terms of a career track. That's part of the reason I do the kind of work I do. My wife, fortunately, attends almost all the same meetings I do, so that doesn't create a conflict for us. We met working together on anti-war stuff, and part of what made our relationship work was our shared commitment to the same values. Fortunately for me, that's not a conflict.

Other persisters confronted with competing demands solved the problem by sleeping less and working harder. For example, Nancy taught full-time while carrying a full load of movement responsibilities. Strongly committed to both, her solution was simple. "I just stayed up a lot longer to do what I had to do. I have not felt that my peace work had to be reduced because I worked, or vice versa."

Among the shifters, competing responsibilities were not a reason for their leaving the movement. For example, Beth described her life commitments as complementary during the time she was a peace activist. She saw her career as a therapist as part of her peace action and the demands of family had declined because her children were grown, giving her more time for peace activism. On the other hand, Philip experienced considerable tension between leading a peace group and his full-time corporate career. He told of receiving intrusive telephone calls at work. His workplace was rather public and his colleagues were aware that the calls were unrelated to his job. Consequently, he resigned from his leadership position after a year, although he continued as a board member. In this case, the demands of career overtook his interest in peace issues. He handled the problem by scaling down rather than terminating his involvement in the movement.

Among the dropouts, three were influenced to leave peace activism because of competing demands. Monica had a divorce to contend with and was disillusioned with the leader of her group. With personal issues in her life requiring attention and upset about her peace group, she ceased to be active. Ron developed a successful career as a mediator and stopped his peace activism to concentrate on that. Helen gave up her peace activities in order to spend more time with her daughter and to pursue a law degree and a new career. In these cases, competing responsibilities could not be successfully balanced and activism ceased.

Unlike the dropouts, persisters succeeded in balancing the various demands on their time. This success was due in part to less pressure from competing responsibilities. Activists working less than full time or who were retired had more time to devote to movement projects. Family demands fell as children grew to adulthood. Many persisters identified balanced and mutually reinforcing responsibilities as the key to their success as activists. Because peace action was central for them, they consciously organized their lives with this balance and mutual reinforcement in mind. They brought that about through the choices they made. If certain responsibilities hindered their peace work, they were altered or dropped.

CONCLUSION

The commitment of these activists was reinforced by the support of others, both from within and outside their peace communities. Opposition to their peace efforts was generally weak, originating mainly with distant relatives. Their other life demands also tended to be aligned with their peace careers. Among these factors, the presence or absence of competing responsibilities appeared to be significant, more so than either support or opposition. These relationships are shown in Figure 6.1.

The stories revealed that involvement in peace action produces its own base of support within the peace community. A peace worker can expect strong backing from fellow activists over time. Because of the generally altruistic nature of peace efforts, support also seemed to develop quite naturally among an activist's immediate family and close friends, who, though not engaged in peace activism themselves, respected others who were. There was also a degree of ideological agreement among members of a family and between friends, because they tended to have similar beliefs and common perceptions about life.

Figure 6.1: Factors Reinforcing Commitment

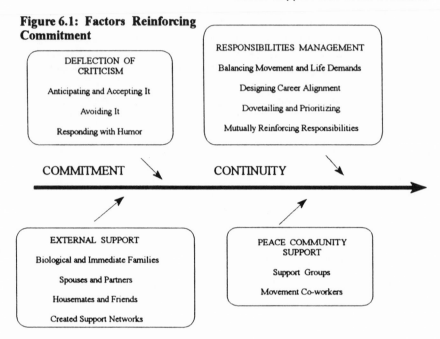

Also, through the self-selection process, activists were inclined to alter their friendship patterns so that their closest friends were either other activists or people whose beliefs were sympathetic to peace and social justice.

While some experienced opposition to their peace activism, it was moderate and, because it often came from geographically distant relatives, it was discounted. In addition, they expected opposition because of the nature of their work and, being certain of their beliefs, they were unmoved by it. Had there been a case where strong opposition came from a significant other in an activist's life, the response might have been different.

None of our respondents shifted to other movements or dropped out of activism because they lacked social support, or because their commitment was under heavy attack from others. Support did exist and opposition was minimal. However, in three cases, peace activism was adversely affected by competing demands: Monica, Ron, and Helen dropped out to take care of other pressing matters. So, pressures from other areas of a person's life do make a substantial difference. Activist commit-ment levels seem to be affected by the nature of their whole system of life obligations.

7

STRATEGIES OF PERSISTENCE

Support from friends, family, and other social contacts motivated these activists to continue striving for a just and peaceful world. Still, by its very nature, peace action must inevitability lead to periods of disappointment and exhaustion. How do persisters, individually and collectively, overcome those risks of the activist trade? How do they hang on when the forces of mainstream society appear to work so actively against them and their vision?

To understand their ways of coping, we will first look at the settings, events, and difficulties that produce the weariness and strain on commitment commonly referred to in social movements as burnout. Most of this chapter will be devoted to the main strategies our persisters devised for withstanding those stresses, then we will address the question of whether our shifters and dropouts left the movement because of burnout.

BURNOUT

Burnout is a term commonly used by social activists. It may vary in intensity and duration. In its most extreme form, it is a condition where an activist has expended all of his or her physical and emotional resources. This produces a sudden collapse of effort, since there is no further personal energy to invest in movement activities. The ambition, hope, and commitment that existed just a day or two earlier suddenly disappear. This condition most often arises after a prolonged period of intense activity. For one person, burnout might have followed a Rocky Flats demonstration which had taken months to prepare and then was poorly received by the mainstream media and the public. For another, burnout may have resulted from a prolonged period of organizational conflict within a peace group. A third might become totally discouraged by a sudden increase in public support for war or nuclear weapons. In the face of such events, some activists might exit from the movement, turn to other commitments they had put aside, or continue movement work mechanically but ineffectively.

Through experience, persisters learned how to develop strategies for coping with burnout so they were not overwhelmed by it to the point where they wanted to leave peace activism for good. For instance, one tactic many described was building a support group, a community of other peace activists to whom they could turn when they were at the end of their personal resources. For instance, Michael avoided reaching "that place of despair. I have created enough support that I don't get terribly blue and discouraged and want to quit it all." While burnout does affect persisters in numerous ways, they learned how to handle it effectively.

Discouragement in Time and Place

Persisters described their periods of waning commitment as variously cyclical, personal, and brought on by the prospect of overwhelming challenges. Rebecca noticed "real cycles to it," where first commitment decreases, but then "it's just a matter of time before I find the right niche and I can just be soaring again with lots of energy." Others spoke of mood swings which sometimes led to depression. In those commitment "valleys," doubt crept in. Matt remembered moments when he fell into despair as he thought about how little had been accomplished on the peace front. At that point, he would question whether he was too idealistic and whether he should just face the reality of the situation and quit it all. "There's that temptation," he said, "of a solid job and a retirement plan and all that stuff. So far I've resisted, but there's been a voice that haunts me once in a while."

Persisters inevitably reversed this decline in energy and commitment. They got a "second wind," sometimes when a new opportunity presented itself. For example, a decision at Rocky Flats to begin incinerating nuclear waste helped Don rekindle his commitment by promising a new challenge with "meaning" and "significance." For a renewal of commitment of this kind, the new challenge had to be met with a sense of inner motivation.

Just as commitment appeared to go through cycles over time, it responded to certain kinds of conditions as well. Work overload was a common problem for persisters but some, like Sally, seemed especially vulnerable to it. "That's when I become weary, when I've taken on too much." Others stretched their limits by trying to carry their projects through to perfection. Allen spoke about this problem, recalling an aid caravan to El Salvador he organized. In the early stages of the project, he felt a need to put a lot of energy and time into it, because for that country and that time, it was the ideal project. Trying to make this project work perfectly made heavy demands on his personal resources.

For others, weariness came about primarily from dealing with interpersonal conflicts within the movement. Lynn found those conflicts to be the most frustrating part of her peace activism. Asking the world to make peace in light of the movement's own deficiencies in internal peacekeeping required special energy from her.

> There have been times when I thought the people that I saw engaged in the peace world were less peaceful than most and less willing to really work on interpersonal peace. It made me feel a little crazy. How can I be asking these people who are working on this nuclear trigger device at Rocky Flats to stop doing what they're doing when apparently we're not able to make peace among ourselves?

The discouragement arising from this kind of tension within peace organizations might drive an activist from a specific group but rarely from the movement. As Joan put it: "I've thought about dropping out of a particular group but I don't feel like I would stop doing peace work. I think, well, why should I do it in this group if it's such a hassle? I can do this work better in another place."

Sometimes the problem was not that activists were working at cross purposes, one against another, but simply that they were unwilling to cooperate or provide support for each other on a common project. When Rebecca left one organization for another it was for this reason. She could not find other activists who were willing to support or enter into her project and, because she did not have "enough energy to create it alone," she quit that group. Allen also became discouraged and left peace action because he did not feel supported by his movement colleagues. Their criticism of his leadership style, including charges he was being authoritarian and sexist, led him to a point where he could no longer take risks within the organization. Used to being judged by his political opponents on the right but not by his peace compatriots, he felt vulnerable and isolated. This led him first to become more withdrawn, then to eventually drop out.

COPING STRATEGIES

Whatever the dynamics and conditions of burnout persisters confronted, they found ways to either deter it or bring themselves out of it. Those strategies drew heavily on their core beliefs and goals, and certain features of their personalities.

Balance

As they discussed their experience with burnout control, persisters emphasized the importance of balance as a rule for healthy living. Balance for Michael included "eating healthily, sleeping well, working hard, meditation, some kind of spiritual discipline, associations with others, keeping your sense of balance, not letting yourself get overextended." Sally said balance was an important element in "learning to take care of myself." This learning process included emotional health, such as discovering how to handle her feelings openly and honestly.

Caring for their physical well-being was a coping device frequently mentioned by persisters as a way of sustaining themselves and of keeping tension at a manageable level in order to avoid burnout. Physical exercise appeared time and again in persisters' stories as a tactical antidote to activist fatigue and depression. These physical diversions took many forms, including mountain hiking, competitive sports, birding, walking, and Tai Chi.

Diversity

Diversity of experience was another aspect of sustainable living for persisters. They sought a rich mix of experiences in their lives. In addition to physical exercise, they also tried to vary their work, played just for the fun of it, took on new challenges to avoid stagnation, and spent time in natural settings in order to return to a larger perspective. Matt found renewal in nature.

> For myself, it's been necessary to have these other areas of engagement that enrich my life, that offer avenues for intuition and wisdom

in order to appreciate the beauty of the world, which has reinforced my commitment in subtle ways. To take time to see why I was working for peace regularly, like how wonderful this earth is and how extravagantly beautiful when you just walk up the canyon here. It seems everything is in bloom.

Creativity

Another way persisters avoided burnout was to engage in creative endeavors. Some people found gardening a great release, whether it was raising vegetables or giving their house plants more attention. Others spent more creative time with their children to recover some of the personal meaning in their lives. Still others made music or quilts, wrote autobiographies or poetry, went back to their looms to weave, took up places at their easels and created visual art. These journeys back into creativity renewed their energies, sense of meaning, and hope at a time when the frustrations and disappointments of peace action weighed heavily upon them. If they felt at risk of burning out, the creative act helped to prevent it. If they were burned out, creativity helped to renew their spirit.

Patience

Some persisters prevented burnout by cultivating patience, a stoic outlook that permitted them to withstand failures by knowing that their peace efforts would eventually pay off. Susan's experience illustrated this beautifully. She spent a great deal of time canvassing door to door for her group, an activity which would test the tenacity of any committed activist.

> You'll go for weeks without talking to anyone who's nice to you. You'll finally break down and just sit on the curb. This has happened to me a lot. And I knock on the next door, and it's like, "Come on in, sit down and talk for a while," and they give you a big check or lots of encouragement. If you stick with it, you make it.

Some persisters drew this patience from a larger vision, like Sally's perception of a never ending effort at world improvement that is "chipping away at the structure and attempting to empower people so that they will say, 'this isn't good enough for us'."

In these accounts of patience, there is the realization that what peace activists are doing today may only bear fruit for future generations. Theirs is a willingness to work within a more profound vision of the future which keeps them going, even in the face of disappointments and burnout. One way they coped with collapses of energy and will was to return to this broader picture, which put their immediate situation into a context they could handle. Remembering the peace vision and returning to it during tough times was one way they overcame their weariness.

Silence and Solitude

Most persisters found renewal in silence and solitude. Being quiet and alone gave them time for reflection, when they could regain their perspective and get back in touch with the fundamentals. Matt found it essential "just being quiet within oneself to restore the flow of energy and commitment that we need." Meditation, silent worship in Quaker meeting, and backpacking alone in remote areas were common tactics in our persisters' burnout strategies. One even found renewal in the ominous silence near Ground Zero on the Nevada Test Site shortly before a nuclear detonation.

Association

For persisters, the therapeutic value of solitude was matched by the joy of being with others in relaxed settings. "Celebrating" is a term used by activists to describe group activity within the movement—playing music, going to a film or play, enjoying a sense of community by just having fun together. It was often through such associations that persisters found emotional release in the sharing of humor, anger, disappointment, and a life path that is often difficult. Being with others in this way encouraged a renewal of faith in and commitment to the peace-building enterprise.

Close ties with "significant others" who were also travelers on the peace journey helped to prevent burnout. Many persisters consciously developed support groups with whom they could air their feelings and encourage each other. This helped to keep their tension levels within a tolerable range and renewed their commitment. For Matt, finding a life partner who supported his peace activism made a difference.

> I talk about my activism with my wife, and she's been very supportive and has really been the biggest blessing in my life. I didn't think

there was another person around who would want to suffer simplicity the way I define it. She had an entirely different family experience, so it's wonderful to have that dialogue. And I do as much good for her with my own feedback, so we hold each other up.

Acceptance of material simplicity as a rule for living seemed to help persisters develop more satisfying human relationships, because their emphasis tended to be less on things and more on people. This appreciation for relationships that "really work" enabled them to establish better connections with others. They were more able to face disappointment and exhaustion because others, like Matt's wife, were always "on call" for burnout prevention and recovery.

Development of Self

At the core of these strategies for dealing with burnout was a conscious effort on the part of persisters to create a way of being, thinking, and feeling that would sustain their peace commitments. This was the life design effort they undertook to preserve their movement commitments while maintaining personal equilibrium. In fact, any reflective person might consider following a similar course in order to move through life with less stress. This would include: Cultivating self-knowledge, understanding one's essential needs and balancing them, even becoming aware of those same needs in others; adjusting one's expectations to the difficulty of realizing a life vision; responding in a healthy way to the disappointments of rewards hoped for but not received; learning how to get away, rest, say no without guilt, pace oneself so play is interspersed with work, and to be gentle with others and oneself.

SHIFTERS, DROPOUTS, AND BURNOUT

Although neither shifters nor dropouts specifically mentioned burnout as a reason for leaving the peace movement, we cannot say with confidence that burnout did not play a role. Burnout is an explanation people may use when they reach a certain point of exhaustion or disappointment. Burnout based on disappointment may begin to appear as statements, such as, "I'm fed up," "I can't take it anymore," or "Since I'm not appreciated, I'm going to leave." If we think of burnout only as physical and emotional exhaustion, then none of our shifters and dropouts left for that reason. But other issues caused them sufficient irritation to appear similar to burnout, such as Beth's disappointment with the leadership of the Rocky Mountain Peace Center, Monica's disillusionment with the leader of her peace group, and Allen's feeling of rejection by the peace organization he had faithfully served.

When circumstances lead activists to question their involvement in a peace group, the idea of burnout may arise to facilitate leaving. "I'm burning out" may be the justification which makes exit possible, whether it emerges from physical exhaustion, emotional collapse, or disappointment about something that has occurred within their peace communities. Although our evidence is not clear on this point, it is possible that burnout did affect shifters and dropouts. While they did not mention it as a reason for leaving, it may have been working in the background as a possible cause for a change in their commitment.

CONCLUSION

Persisters handled the problems of declining energies, discouragement, and temporary burnout with coping strategies which prevented the loss of faith and confidence that often lead the less committed to abandon peace action. The intensity of their commitment did fluctuate over time; they experienced mood swings and temporary burnout was not uncommon. Usually, this occurred after periods of intense effort, followed by disappointing results. Under these circumstances, they were forced to suspend their peace activities briefly in order to recover their energy and sense of balance, but they did not experience the "exit burnout" of others. Each developed coping strategies for overcoming burnout which enabled them to persevere: Balance of action and reflection, of work and play; diversity to prevent stagnation and boredom; creativity to show the way to new possibilities and personal expression; continual reconnection with nature and children; patience rooted in a vision of peace which they knew would not be realized in their lifetimes but which they nevertheless pursued; the use of silence and solitude to restore the sense of inner peace so necessary for continuing commitment; association with kindred souls that provided a sense of community; and development of self as part

Figure 7.1: Persister Burnout Strategies

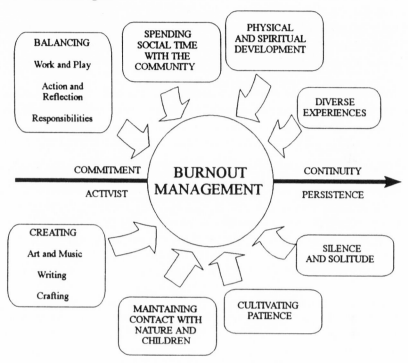

of a larger life search for a successful way to live in a world full of tension and short on meaning. These strategies appear in Figure 7.1.

The coping strategies of activists are an important theoretical focus, for researchers have paid scant attention to how members of movements manage their commitments in creative ways. It is striking how much creativity these activists used in this process. They organized their lives so activism was possible, then constantly devised ways to keep it going, even when life circumstances were stretching them to the limit. Coping strategies are among the larger number of creative choices they made during their protest careers, as their stories revealed time and again.

For theory-building, the creative coping strategies of these activists can expand our thinking about the range of forces which shape and drive collective action. For activism in the field, they pose some practical questions. Of what use are these strategies to the peace movement as a whole? Can they be taught as one might teach community organizing? If so, could a conscious effort to teach them produce more persistence and a healthier movement?

8

ACTIVISM AND PERSONAL GROWTH

The success of persisters in deterring and overcoming burnout is inextricably connected with a carefully examined life and a fair amount of self-awareness. It does not emerge from a book or a workshop but from living a life of peace action, making creative choices, and learning how to persist. By walking the line between the heavy demands of activism and the threat of burnout, they are able to maintain their commitment to a vision of social change in which peace and more equitable sharing of resources are crucial goals. That vision is a compelling image of the change they are working so hard to achieve. Yet, there is another level of change they seldom talked about—their own personal development.

When asked how their peace activism had affected their personal growth, some were surprised at the question. They were simply not accustomed to thinking about how they benefited personally from their movement experience. However, many welcomed the opportunity to reflect on the question, never having thought seriously about it before. Their reflections testify to the personal impact activism can have on people in peace careers. How they developed personally as a consequence of their activism is what we explore in this chapter.

PERSONAL CHANGES

Peace activists fail to speak of their personal growth partly because of their sharp focus on social issues and partly because of their concern for community, which places less emphasis on individualism and more on communal issues and social change. By our asking respondents to discuss the personal changes they experienced as a result of their peace work, a neglected dimension of social activism was revealed.

What we learned about those changes casts the peace movement in a new light. It becomes not only a collective effort to diminish violence in the world, but also a vehicle for personal evolution. While these personal changes are a residual effect of the activist's commitment to changing the world, they are important nonetheless for explaining what keeps people involved in activism over many years. They are unrecognized selective incentives which help to keep activists committed.

Self-Empowerment

Activism provides many opportunities for taking risks, by participating in demonstrations, being arrested, speaking in front of groups, writing unpopular tracts, or simply standing out from the crowd. Activists are continually being tested personally. During nonviolent demonstrations where arrests and retaliation may be possible, they must summon the courage to act in the face of fear. Rebecca described her activism as the chief cause of her personal development because it forced her to face fears and take risks. The question which kept surfacing for her was: "It's time to face this, what's holding you back?" As she put it: "I don't know how one can really make developmental changes and move forward until there is a barrier to be overcome which forces you to ask: 'Why can't I go on, what am I afraid of?'"

Activism challenged Rebecca, and others, to do things they had never done before and to face the risk of public antagonism. It was a test of character and it strengthened them. Again and again, overcoming fear through these acts of courage helped to build inner strength. They referred to this as self-empowerment, or having the self-confidence to carry out a plan of action effectively, however risky it might seem.

Skills in Communicating and Organizing

Part of the self-empowerment of these activists occurred around the development of specific skills. The two areas of growth most often mentioned were learning how to communicate and how to organize effectively. Peace activism provides frequent opportunities for communication—speaking before groups and at rallies, defending the peace vision in public debates, writing about peace and social justice issues for newspapers and newsletters. From their movement experience they learned to write more clearly, became more confident public speakers and deepened their capacity to listen.

Arlene spoke about developing more confidence as a communicator. She had found speaking in public a traumatic experience when she was younger. Her activism required her to speak about peace issues at elementary schools, book clubs, service groups like Kiwanis and Rotary, retirement homes, and city council meetings. Called upon to speak often, she eventually overcame her fear of public speaking. Now, she says, there is "no fear at all, no quaking."

These activists also felt that developing organizational skills significantly influenced their personal development. Don spoke of learning how to conduct a meeting, how to plan, how to draw people out, how "to develop consensus where people work together in decision-making, as opposed to majority rule where you have winners and losers." The continuing need to build consensus in the movement made him more sensitive to others and better able to listen carefully to different points of view. He learned a new organizing style, of facilitating a group rather than leading it with a definite plan he would try to convince others to follow. The consensus-building process taught him how to follow as well as lead. He grew personally from this new way of thinking about leadership and building agreement among people.

Developing a Broader Perspective

Working cooperatively with others can lead one to become more tolerant of different points of view and to appreciate cultural and political diversity. Several activists spoke of cultivating this broader perspective on life in their movement work. Brian mentioned becoming more aware of people's points of view and ways of life as a result of working with an "incredible variety of people" from different social classes, religions, and ethnic backgrounds. Working side by side with so many different kinds of people gave these activists a clearer picture of a multi-cultural future, where people of various backgrounds would live in harmony without the social distinctions which currently separate them.

Relationship with Others

The peace movement has been a school for its members in the sense that it has taught them new ways of relating to others. A greater appreciation of cultural diversity is one sign of this change; there is also evidence of increasing sensitivity to how people should treat one another. Persisters especially emphasized that learning new ways of relating to others was an important personal change for them. They became more understanding and sensitive to people, more loving, less judgmental, and more patient. Sally spoke of becoming "more compassionate and less afraid of people." Her peace activism forced her to move beyond her fear and to reach out to others. Sometimes this meant having more compassion for those who opposed her peace efforts, to understand rather than hate them.

Gandhi and King were important influences on the thinking of these activists. Committed to the ways of nonviolence these leaders advocated, which emphasized "loving your enemy," they understood the need for compassion, of going beyond the apparent differences between people to see what lies at the core—a profound similarity of spirit. This training in compassion added something to their personal development—the capacity for affection—so that the divisions of class, race, and political disagreements could be avoided or overcome.

Emotional Maturity

One does not develop compassion overnight. There is an inner struggle that must be undertaken against one's baser emotions, such as hatred and the desire for revenge. So, it was no surprise to hear activists speak about these struggles and the changes they were ultimately able to make in their emotional lives.

Numerous persisters discussed changes in their emotional tendencies as a consequence of their peace activism. Matt mentioned a reduction of anger and fear. He described carrying a "big burden of anger" and learning how to acknowledge it in himself but "not to let it run around loose and hurt other people." Managing his anger made more room for positive feelings and led him to believe that humans are not compelled to live out of the limitations of their childhood personalities. They can change. "We do learn, we can go on, we can do things differently and make better sense of our lives."

Knowing that he could change gave Matt faith that our society can change. "As deep as the roots of violence in our society go," he said, "I think that the roots we can cultivate with each other can go deeper in a nonviolent way and can replace violence. It has to do with learning about life and learning about yourself and how you can work with other people."

This comment is an appeal for greater awareness, for learning about ourselves at deeper levels, especially our fears, hatred, and appetite for power. Matt would say that we must then try to transform those emotions into something more constructive, or at least keep them in check. This is a major challenge many of these activists have been undertaking in their personal lives. It is a difficult but necessary task, according to Matt, if society is to change at a fundamental level.

How this change might be achieved was suggested by Lynn, a woman who gave up a secure position in social work to live with and serve the poor.

> When I had a social work career, it was a lot of battering away at people to change something. I think people need to be affirmed and loved and invited to think about other possibilities, not coerced or badgered. When I was a teenager I was sort of argumentative, but I've dropped a lot of the judgmental stuff and the notion that my way is the only way. So it's a sort of maturing that I think the nonviolence movement has produced in me—how to deal with anger, how to make decisions, and how to affirm people with whom you disagree. All of those things feel to me like a good evolution in my personal life.

Here the message seems clear: People seeking to change the structures of society need to work at two levels. They must work diligently to change the structures directly, but they must also do the inner work of changing themselves. As Lynn said, this is the power of nonviolence, using it not simply as a strategy for action but as a way of understanding the self and how to transform it.

Life Style Changes

Life style changes occur for many who are deeply involved in the peace movement. Matt mentioned leading a more nonviolent life. Grant spoke about his peace activism as shaping his life goals, the way he lives, his spirituality, the way he relates to his church, family, and friends. Susan began to lead a more radical life and Arlene mentioned shifting her life toward friendships, realizing "the importance of other people, of loyalty, and the role of a sense of humor."

Jennifer described the peace movement as a place where she learned a new model of living. People she grew up with are now in successful careers, making "lots of money." She took a different route, a life devoted to service, to peace and social justice. This has meant living at the margin, with a very low salary and long working hours. This has made her an "outsider." "When you make a choice to be an activist for these peace and justice issues, unfortunately that puts you outside of a lot of mainstream things in this culture. And you have to come to terms with that and feel comfortable with it."

Jennifer's peace activism has given her an alternative set of role models and values for making this outsider role acceptable to her. It has not been easy, for an activist's life is set against the mainstream and is thus removed from the usual sources of admiration and social status. The activist chooses to be an outsider, not because there is something inherently satisfying about sacrifice, but because the issues are so important. It is this sense of urgency which drives the activist outside the mainstream.

One of the functions of the peace movement is to offer another way of organizing society and human relationships. The mission is like a calling, with a force of its own, drawing the person to make sacrifices in the name of larger purposes, of bigger dreams that only outsiders can dream. It is always the outsiders who want to change society in dramatic ways, for they have dreamt the dream that shapes the future in a way quite different from the past.

More Meaning

While the outsider status has its costs, there are rewards within social activism as well. One of those is meaning. The activist's calling gives life purpose, as Martha noted. "I would like to think I'm healthier because I have ideas that I consider wholesome and that are moving me in a direction I want to go in, rather than being at loose ends, not knowing what I'm doing or why I'm doing it." The meaning of Martha's life emerged from her social activism as she spent some time each day taking action on the issues of peace or social justice. "Every day I look at my calendar and see what I'm doing and look at my pile of correspondence from all those groups that are going to go broke if I don't send them money."

When one is serving a larger purpose than simply acquiring money, social status, and power, there is deeper meaning in life. What peace activists do seems to them to make more difference in humanity's positive evolution. Acts undertaken for the calling, however small, have deeper significance. This meaning affects a person's development, giving life added depth and breadth.

Becoming a More Complete Person

Peace work helped these activists become more complete, which, in their view, meant greater attention to improving themselves and becoming more informed citizens. Susan said:

> The more I learn and educate myself on what's going on in the world, the more I realize how many things I need to do and to work on personally. The more I work on those things, the better person I become. I'm not going to be perfect, I'm still racist and sexist and all that, but I think I become less so the more I work at it.

The concept of "better person" is a matter of perspective. What these activists meant by "better" follows the discourse of non-violence in a context of global change. Being a better listener, more loving, more compassionate, more aware, more patient—these are aspects of personal "goodness" in their eyes. Yet, as Susan recognized, one must keep in mind what must still be done about racism and sexism. In their stories, there was a noticeable absence of the "Pollyanna" mentality and the inflated ego. They understood that they engage in peace action out of conviction and that the struggle will be hard and long. They were also aware that they still have issues to resolve within themselves.

Part of becoming a better person is being more informed as a citizen. This was regarded by several activists as a personal change. For instance, June credited the peace movement with expanding her knowledge of world issues. "I've opened my eyes a little bit. I'm more aware of the broader world and I think my peace activism has helped me do that. Even though it's just a little step, it's helped me a lot personally." Being a more informed person is as much a goal as an achievement for persisters, because they know that there are always new issues to learn about. This never ending process has been a source of personal development for some of these people.

Greater Acceptance of "What Is"

Peace activists operate from a vision of the future and a system of beliefs that motivate them to take responsibility and act. Yet, they know their undertaking is difficult, and that desired change occurs slowly and will take generations to achieve. They have learned how to live with this reality and their many disappointments. David made this point.

> Since 1978, my peace activism has been my personal development. It's been learning to live with the disappointment and disillusionment, that it isn't going to be this wonderful, loving, supportive place but that I have to deal with the in-fighting, living with the defeats, and with the fact that nothing essentially has changed and things have definitely gotten a lot worse during my lifetime. My personal development has been learning to cope with this emotionally, growing enough so that I can do that.

There is a taoist tone in David's understanding, of continuing the action while not resisting what you get. For peace activists, this hard lesson, once learned, keeps their commitment from giving way to despair.

Greater Ethical Clarity

Peace activists continually face disappointment, yet they keep at the work. What motivates them is not success, for that is rare. Rather, it is their beliefs and deep sense of ethics. A few began their lives in families where moral outrage at social injustice helped set their direction. Others, such as Brian, achieved more ethical clarity through their activism. "Doing this work has helped me to focus on my own ethical and political philosophy, to explain to myself and to other people why I'm doing this."

Grant talked about the importance of living a "life of integrity." What he meant was clear: Each person has to live in harmony with essential values. Integrity comes not from succeeding in what one undertakes, although that cannot be ignored, but in remaining faithful to one's ethical roots. That faith gives a certain beauty to that individual's life. You can tell "who people are" by the nature of their ethical commitments, Grant said, "that's ultimately what it comes down to." Learning to live life with integrity, in the face of disappointment, was one notable element in the personal development of these activists.

Greater Inner Peace

A number of these activists are seeking inner peace as they go about the business of creating a more peaceful world. Jack was one of those living at the intersection of personal and world peace. For example, he appreciated the use of silence when conflict rather than common purpose was dominating a meeting. He also preferred that peace demonstrations be quiet, with a sense of meditation. "I get pretty troubled about peace demonstrators going down the street screaming and shaking their fists. I tend to distance myself from that kind of peace activity because I think the peace is missing there."

Jack was seeking a connection between peace action and his own personal center. This life-long goal has been elusive.

I don't view myself as a paragon of peace, you know, of personal peace. There's so much of a tendency for peacemakers to come out of a sense of injustice, seeing injustices that are around and becoming disturbed about it and disturbed is a short distance from angry, and angry is a short distance from getting violent, whether it's physical or not. When you are a peace person, the challenge is to keep the action peaceful and thus keep the message alive.

Jack's effort to create peace within himself as he does movement work is shown in his current effort to help prison inmates develop inner peace as they seek to renounce violence. Through various techniques, he trains prisoners to deal with the fear, rage, and consequent conflict which often lead them into trouble. This program is a way "of teaching a kind of inner peace, a way of coping with potential violence and turning it around into a peaceful situation." Jack does the inner work so the outer peace work can remain faithful to its essential mission.

Attaining inner peace, a major challenge of conscious living, is as difficult as working for peace in the world. Integrating the personality, or what Jung called "individuation,"[1] leads ultimately to peace within—a goal of all world religions. Yet, like world peace, struggling for and committing oneself to the goal's realization is what is important, for, without effort, nothing is accomplished. What is not dreamt, cannot be sought. What is not sought can never be attained.

If we live in the broader time perspective these activists have chosen, such goals are not unrealistic, simply difficult to achieve. For persisters like Jack, inner peace and world peace are interconnected goals and the movement is the incubator for those possibilities.

THE PSYCHOLOGICAL DEVELOPMENT OF PEACE ACTIVISTS

Those interested in developing citizens oriented toward nonviolence, peace, and social justice must confront the question of socialization: What kind of person is likely to have a long term commitment to peace and social justice? To answer this question more needs to be known about the psychological make-up of persistent activists, although that dimension cannot be separated from the important social influences which shape their commitments.

This line of inquiry is undertaken by David Adams in his interesting book, *Psychology for Peace Activists*.[2] He examines the lives of ten leading activists for peace and social justice.[3] Six stages of their psychological development are identified which appeared to set them off from others: Acquisition of values and purpose, anger, action, affiliation, personal integration, and world-historic consciousness.

The acquisition of values and purpose grows out of early life experiences in the family and church, where the child becomes politically conscious about peace and social justice. These values are further developed through action. What works against peace and justice values and purpose is alienation, the sense of being alone and in despair about having a personal effect on social and political conditions.

Anger motivates someone with this psychological development to take action. The person must be sufficiently upset about the political arrangement of society to move from passivity into action. "Not all anger is useful for consciousness and development," Adams notes. "The anger that can be harnessed to action and consciousness development is anger directed against institutions of war and injustice, rather than anger directed against individuals as such."[4] Fear and pessimism work against such anger.

Adams regards action as the most important phase in the psychological development of a peace activist. One may hold peace and justice values and be angry about injustice, but until she or he decides to take action, that person will simply watch events from the sidelines as an "armchair theorist." Action is not simply a sign that an individual has moved from one stage of development to another: Action, in itself, has the effect of changing the person.

> It is a basic principle of the new psychology that people are transformed by the actions that they initiate. Not only the consequences of the actions, but the very process of taking action changes the actor so that he or she becomes a "new person" operating at a higher level of consciousness. Values and purpose are reinforced. Anger is channeled into activity, rather than turned inward and allowed to fester into pessimism. Pessimism is dispelled by real results.[5]

Affiliating with like-minded others is another step he feels is essential in the psychological development of a peace activist. Being in a community of activists overcomes atomism and individualism and thus reinforces action, but it does more: It socializes activists further, leading them to an even higher stage of conscious development. In community, people learn to be patient, to compromise, and to be generous—all essential psychological traits for maintaining a commitment to peace and social justice work.

To maintain commitment over a long period, an activist's values, purpose, anger, action, and affiliation must be brought into harmony with the rest of life, including family, friendship, and work, through what Adams calls "personal integration." Without this integration, activists burn out, and, in despair, withdraw from activism. "Sustaining a lifetime of personal action and involvement requires a network of personal support."[6]

For Adams, the final step in the development of the persistent peace activist is the achievement of "world-historic consciousness." This kind of awareness grows out of the challenge of aligning one's efforts with the demands of the historical moment.

World-historic consciousness, the highest step of consciousness, is not the quality of an individual acting alone, but of a leader working in affiliation. It is the kind of leadership that enables action and affiliation for peace and justice to develop in an effective and progressive rather than a narrow and sectarian direction. It's the ability of a leader to know the mood of the people, to analyze the strengths and directions of all political forces, and to organize and broaden the political character of the movement so that it is in step with the agenda of history, which, in the present time, means the abolition of war.[7]

Although he is speaking specifically of leadership here, this type of conscious commitment is something any activist can develop—a sense of personal responsibility for humanity's improvement and the fate of the earth. This supranational consciousness lifts activism into the global context and orients it toward the moral evolution of the species. One who accepts this mission has aligned with the forces of historical development and feels challenged to create a set of social and political arrangements supporting peace and nonviolence and a sustainable future for the planet. Adams sees this global consciousness as the final stage in the psychological development of the peace activist.

The accounts of our peace activists generally confirm Adams' insights. Most were influenced by family, church, and school to embrace the values of peace and social justice. All had become critical of existing institutions, mainly as a result of their education in family or school. Many had personal experiences which led them to believe that social institutions were not working to benefit humankind. All had been turned toward activism and had their consciousness shaped by it, many by the events sweeping the U.S. during the civil rights movement and the Vietnam War. Most had become affiliated with other peace activists and had found those ties important for preserving their commitment. All had found creative ways of integrating their peace activism into their broader lives, reducing social pressures which might have undermined their commitment. Finally, all had developed world consciousness, a commitment to furthering peace and social justice and to preserving the health of the planet for future generations.

CONCLUSION

The personal development of persisters was advanced in various ways as they went about the business of pursuing peace and social justice in the world. Figure 8.1 shows the various ways they changed. The self-assessments of personal change by these activists suggest but a superficial picture of how they as a group differ psychologically from non-activists. A comparative study of the psychology of the two groups would be interesting and would make a significant contribution to our knowledge of the effects of social movement activity on the personal development of activists. Apart from David Adams' work, this has been a largely neglected field of study. We hope our findings serve to elevate the issue of personal development to a more prominent place in collective action research.

Figure 8.1: Personal Growth Rewards of Activism

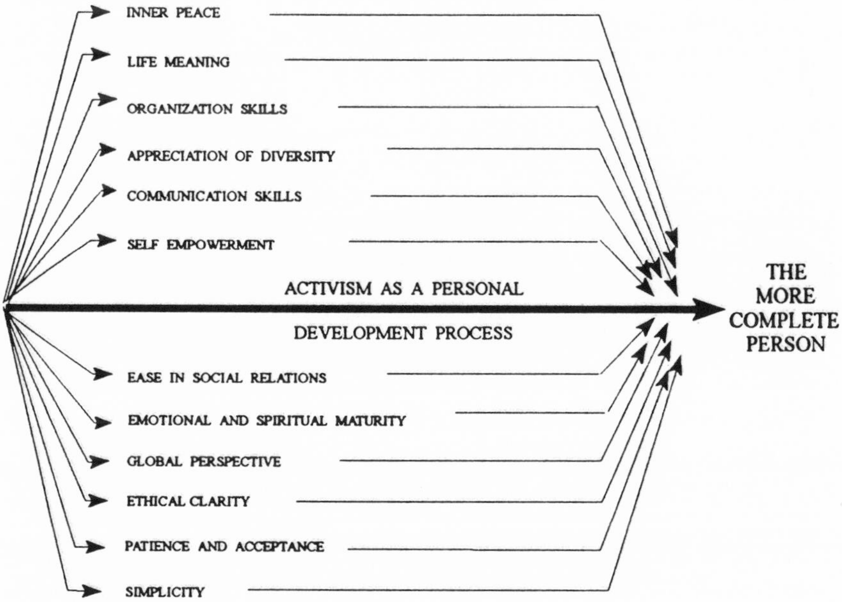

NOTES

1. To understand the human challenge entailed in the process of individuation, we recommend reading Carl G. Jung, *Mysterium Coniunctionis*, Volume XX of his Collected Works. (Princeton, NJ: Princeton University Press, 1970), his commentary in Richard Wilhelm, *Secret of the Golden Flower*. (New York: Harcourt, Brace and World, Inc., 1931), and Jolande Jacobi, *The Way of Individuation*. (New York: New American Library, 1967). It was Jung's view that the integration of the psyche, the achievement of wholeness through the individuation process, produces the sense of inner peace sought within the world's religions.

2. David Adams, *Psychology for Peace Activists: A New Psychology for the Generation Who Can Abolish War*. (New Haven, CT: The Advocate Press, 1989).

3. He studied Eugene Debs, Helen Caldicott, Sandy Pollack, Jane Addams, Emily Balch, Dorothy Day, Bertrand Russell, W.E.B. DuBois, Martin Luther King, Jr., and A.J. Muste.

4. Adams, *op. cit.*, p. 12.

5. *Ibid.*, p. 20.

6. *Ibid.*, p. 30.

7. *Ibid.*, p. 36.

9

HOW PEACE
COMMITMENT SURVIVES

Social movements experience wild fluctuations of membership, often drawing thousands into action during their initial mobilization phase when dreams, anger, and hope are ripe and the excitement of the cause is intoxicating. But over time, other forces come into play, perhaps disillusionment with the dream, frustration with the slowness of change or the movement's leadership, until the thousands dwindle to hundreds. These are the most steadfast and committed who have a different connection to the issues and are determined to stay active indefinitely. They are the persisters.

This study has focused on what makes certain people persist in peace activism when others fall away. While our respondents have been peace and social justice activists, the determinants of commitment we have discovered may improve our understanding of the patterns of activist persistence in other social movements as well. In this chapter, we draw our findings into a theory of sustained commitment.

Developing such a theory is not an easy task. Given the complexity of the relationships to be considered, it can be no more than a best guess about why things happen as they do, or a rough approximation of reality. Even with this limitation, the value of theorizing is that it can open up a dialogue about reality which may clarify the picture as others elaborate upon it.

A THEORY OF SUSTAINED COMMITMENT

We have learned from the stories of our activists that commitments, while they evolve in definite stages, are continually in flux. Thus, our theory lays out stages of commitment, while taking into account the social and personal forces which tend to reinforce and undermine commitments. We speak of "commitment fluctuation," variations of commitment intensity as the dynamics of a person's life alter conditions, demands, and personal motivation. Thus, our theory of sustained commitment is broad for it shows not only how commitment persists but also how it can weaken and eventually collapse.

The Contexts of Activist Commitment

Activist commitments develop within the micromobilization contexts where local peace groups work and the macromobilization arena where national and international events and larger political forces shape local agendas, projects, and opportunities. For example, economic expansion and political liberalization occurring at the national level can have important effects on local activism and commitment. In fact, some persisters supported their peace activism with foundation grants and consulting fees which were not available before the 1980s. Access to previously classified material through the Freedom of Information Act also gave their work a new sense of realism and resolve, as they could then disclose clandestine governmental operations in various parts of the world to prove their claims. "Macro" and "micro" contexts also intersected in the nationally controlled but locally situated military installations whose presence was highly influential in activating commitment over long periods. The presence of such threatening facilities as Rocky Flats stimulated protests which drew thousands of people from many parts of the country and over many years.

Since social movements are responses to problems in society, any theory of sustained commitment must pay attention to the larger context of those strains within and between societies. For peace and social justice activists, those problems encompass the threat of nuclear war, conventional wars, and other forms of violence; environmental degradation; the injustices of poverty, racism, and sexism; and the presence of striking political and social inequalities. These issues are the catalyst for movement formation and the reason activists participate, sometimes in the face of personal risks.

Persisters, shifters, and dropouts became involved in social activism because they felt the issues were significant and the need for a new social and political order was pressing. Individuals in all three groups hoped a new society would emerge which would be nonviolent, egalitarian, and based on social justice for all. Where persisters differed from shifters and dropouts was in their stronger attention to peace and nonviolence issues and their belief that a continuing commitment to peace activism was essential for making the desired changes.

Socialization to Peace-Oriented Beliefs

What a person thinks will determine what is seen, what is known, and what is done. Beliefs—collections of ideas about what is "true"—are the ways that humans orient to the physical world and to each other. As children, we are exposed to the beliefs of our parents and significant others. Through socialization, we internalize those beliefs so gradually that we are unaware that our perceptions of others and the social world are based on the social constructions of our families, churches, and schools. We do not know we have been socialized. Unaware of how we acquired our beliefs, they naturally appear to us as the "truth." It is this confidence in the truth of beliefs which makes them such powerful influences on human action, especially ethical beliefs which prescribe moral behavior, as Jenkins' study of the farm workers movement so clearly shows.[1] Peace activists, like everyone else, are socialized in this way, and they are taught by influential people in their lives to embrace a specific belief system, which encompasses beliefs about the goals of peace and social justice and the importance of using nonviolent means to reach them.

Learning to Help Others. Persisters learned, often at a young age, that helping others was a moral duty. They were taught to "Do unto others as you would have them do unto you." Many absorbed this principle at home and in church. Others learned to empathize with the poor, to understand the social causes of poverty, racism, and sexism, and to feel a comradeship with the oppressed. Simple acts of kindness toward others were encouraged. If these ideas were not adopted early, they were embraced after becoming involved in peace activism. Compassion was the central tenet of this learning process. Without some feeling of compassion, it is unlikely that a peace and social justice commitment will form.

There was no discernible difference in the presence of altruism between persisters, shifters, and dropouts, although we were unable to measure the intensity of their beliefs. What their stories reveal is that altruistic beliefs seem to be a necessary condition for peace activism and that shifters and dropouts are not distinguished from persisters on that dimension. Rather, they differed along other lines: The particular problem focus of their altruism; the strength of their belief that peace action was urgent; and how much they became identified with peace work, became immersed in the peace community, and integrated peace activism into their everyday lives.

Shifters refocused their altruism on social issues other than peace partly because they reached a point where they felt other social issues were more urgent. Some became disillusioned with some aspect of the peace movement and shifted their activism to a different social issue in hopes of finding a group which functioned more in line with their expectations. Dropouts, who also held altruistic beliefs, left the peace movement for a variety of reasons, some having to do with personal crises in their lives or competing responsibilities. There were also a few shifters and dropouts who left because of conflicts within their peace groups, which caused them to be pushed out of peace activism by fellow activists or led them to withdraw as a way of resolving an interpersonal or policy conflict.

Learning to Be Critical of Social Institutions. Family, school, and personal experience taught persisters to challenge the legitimacy of social institutions. For many, the social movements of the 1960s set the tone for this training in social criticism and for learning to "question authority." The movements for civil rights, for peace in Vietnam, and for women's liberation fostered a climate of sharp questioning, especially in our colleges and universities. There, students were taught to think critically about social and global problems and to understand how national policies and priorities were contributing to them. As college students, they learned about war, poverty, oppression and the social institutions that support them. This critical attitude toward social institutions and authority made them angry and indignant toward the political system, which prepared them for activism.

Like altruistic beliefs, resistance to the existing order did not distinguish persisters from shifters and dropouts. All three groups were opposed to many of our government's international and national policies and the social values behind them. They also felt that using conventional political means was unlikely to produce results, because elected representatives were unwilling to make the dramatic leap in thinking and policy which conditions demanded. Disillusioned with normal politics, they came to believe that nonviolent social activism was an alternative way to make the changes the larger systemic problems required.

Political disaffection seems to be a necessary condition for peace activism, for without a strong criticism of existing conditions, policies and procedures, people are unlikely to turn to nonviolent direct action for social change. Persisters used peace activism and social protest tactics as a way of working for change after they became disillusioned with the "system," although many also continued to work for it through normal political channels. Shifters, combining their visions of change and their critical attitude, moved on to other social issues. Still wanting to change the existing order, dropouts returned to a non-movement lifestyle, often under pressure from personal problems, competing commitments, or because they became disillusioned with social activism as a way to make the changes they desired.

Learning to See Activism as Problem-Solving. During the protest decades, people had a variety of approaches to solving social problems. Many ran for political office, organized third parties, and worked within the political system to change it. Others thought that the changes they wanted could only be achieved through social activism and the development of radical alternatives. While some persisters were moderates who avoided radical politics and worked in more conventional ways to change the system, most felt that sweeping political reforms were necessary and that they could be produced by nonviolent means. Without this belief that peace action was a solution, they would not have turned toward peace activism as a way to change the political system. They knew that, given the extraordinary nature of the crisis they perceived, extraordinary means were necessary.

Persisters, shifters, and dropouts were all inclined to believe that social activism was a solution to the problems of war and social injustice. Shifters and dropouts differed from persisters in their reluctance to continue in peace action as a solution. This raises the important question of how personally responsible persisters, shifters, and dropouts felt to work for peace.

Learning to Be Socially Responsible. People can be socialized to help others, feel an urgency for change, see the justification for nonviolent activism, but, unless they feel personally responsible to do something, they may languish in their frustration and fail to become active. The belief "I have a responsibility to solve these problems" is fundamental for the making and the persistence of an activist. Some of our respondents had learned about social responsibility from their parents, but most were taught to "stand up and be counted" during the 1960s and 1970s.

The stories of persisters revealed a strong sense of personal responsibility to work for peace. In fact, both persisters and shifters felt personally responsible. Given their identity as peace activists, persisters felt obligated to work for peace directly; whereas, shifters, whose identities were not as strongly tied to peace, transferred their social responsibility to other issues. Peace was still an important priority for most of them: They simply severed their ties to a peace group and became committed elsewhere. Unlike persisters and shifters, dropouts relinquished responsibility for social activism.

Why people channel their feelings of social responsibility into peace action is not entirely clear. It could stem from the strength of peace as an issue in their belief systems, the extent of their integration into a peace community, or the intensity of their feeling that peace action is urgent.

Learning That Peace Action Was Urgent. The Cold War awakened large numbers to the risk and consequences of nuclear war. The 1960s, 1970s, and 1980s were decades of deep anxiety about the fate of humanity and the earth. Life itself was at stake. For many persisters, this was the backdrop for a range of critical issues—war, violence, class oppression, poverty, racism, sexism, and the environmental crisis. At that historic turning point, action seemed imperative. If the opportunity to make changes was missed, the fate of life on earth could be sealed.

Persisters felt a sense of urgency about peace action. In fact, their belief that peace was an urgent issue remained strong over time, which distinguished them from shifters and dropouts. After the Cold War, shifters were inclined to feel that peace was a less pressing concern, as compared to other social issues. For one shifter, solar energy became more crucial, for another the issue was over-population. Dropouts, too, felt peace issues were less compelling, as projects they led were completed or personal matters demanded their attention. For shifters and dropouts, peace became less important than other social issues, family matters, personal problems, or careers. For persisters, peace remained the urgent issue.

As a group, persisters thought that the end of the Cold War had not fundamentally altered the global conditions which had produced wars, group violence, oppression, and social injustice. A few even regarded peace action as more urgent after the Cold War, as ethnic conflicts erupted in the former Soviet Union and threatening regional conflicts, such as the Gulf War, broke out elsewhere. For them, events following the Cold War signaled an increase of violence while the means for nuclear and biological warfare remained precariously in the hands of national leaders. Perceiving the global situation as unstable, persisters maintained their belief that peace action was necessary and this helped to preserve their commitment.

Socialization and Life Pattern: Becoming Available

People are available to pursue courses of action when they are already socialized to move in that direction (attitudinal availability) and when their life patterns make them free enough in time, money, and energy to devote themselves to it (situational availability).

Attitudinal Availability. The accumulation of a person's life experiences sets the stage for activism. Those experiences establish appropriate beliefs, expressed in attitudes, for pursuing specific courses of action using particular means. Some activist directions are not possible because of what people believe; others are likely. In the case of the peace movement, attitudinal availability is the ethical propensity to pursue peace action because the individual holds beliefs in harmony with the movement's goals and means. Those beliefs must be maintained if peace activism is to survive.

Our activists developed the ethical inclination for peace action because they had been socialized—some early in life and others much later—to hold beliefs which were compatible with the peace movement. Those beliefs included the importance of helping others, the need to change social policy around the issues of peace and social justice, the use of nonviolent protest as one of the ways to make change, the importance of personal responsibility for carrying on activism, and their conviction that peace action was necessary. They were ethically prepared to step into the peace activist role and, once they were securely in that role, those beliefs were reinforced and deepened through their involvement with kindred spirits in the peace community. This immersion into the beliefs of the peace community had the effect of making activists more attitudinally available for longer-term commitments.

Situational Availability. The ethical propensity to pursue a particular form of activism (attitudinal availability) must be accompanied by the ability to act (situational availability) if a strong commitment is to form and stay alive. Situational availability is that freedom to take action which arises from a person's life pattern and how it either facilitates activism or inhibits it. People who are working full-time, married with young children, in debt, or in poor health would be less free to undertake peace action, even if they were ethically predisposed to do so. By comparison, people who are in careers with more flexible time schedules or who live communally would have more time and social support for activism because of their life patterns. So would a healthy person who is unmarried and has no children.

It should not be surprising that so many young people become active in protest politics, for they often have more time to become involved than more established citizens with careers and families. They are not necessarily reliable over the long term, however, because most do want careers, a family, a home and, if they aspire to the American dream of material success, they are unlikely to stay in activism for long. Yet, as the stories of these activists show, some young people choose an alternative life style and plan their lives in other ways to keep their peace commitments going. So, situational availability is something activists can control to some extent. To preserve their commitments, they must arrange their lives so they have time and energy for peace action. This is one of the constant challenges faced by activists who want to stay involved over a lifetime.

We discovered that our persisters were creative in designing their lives so they were free to pursue peace action. Some worked part time or developed careers which gave them time for peace action. Others had retired or were homemakers with spare time for community work. Some postponed marriage and having children. Most developed simple life styles which required only moderate incomes. Some created or joined peace communes where money-making and child-rearing were shared, freeing time for peace and social justice work. In various ways, these activists mapped out their lives so they could remain involved in movement work.

Attitudinal and situational availability are important interlocking concepts for understanding how and why peace commitments form and what keeps them going. By itself, attitudinal availability cannot ensure the development or continuation of a peace commitment. If people with the proper beliefs are not also situationally available, it is unlikely that they will develop long-term careers as peace activists. Because the activist life makes heavy demands on people's time, emotions, and energy and usually provides little or no income, many with the proper beliefs but little time or other resources are not apt to become involved in peace activism or, if they do, they are unlikely to stay active for very long. For activism to persist, attitudinal and situational availability must be continually cultivated by the activists themselves and also by the movement community as it reinforces fundamental beliefs and helps its members arrange their lives so they have enough time and energy for movement work.

Personal Opportunity Structure

For individuals who are free to act, a concrete opportunity must be present in order to transform willingness into action. For example, where people live is important. Someone living in a small midwestern town may be attitudinally and situationally available for peace action but be so far from the physical targets of peace action or from existing peace groups that he or she does nothing. In contrast, our respondents, living in a metropolitan area with numerous military installations nearby, had many opportunities for action within easy reach. Many peace organizations in the area were directing nonviolent action at selected targets, such as the Rocky Flats nuclear weapons plant.

Opportunity refers to the possibilities for action identified by existing peace organizations and those created by activists who initiate their own projects. When these opportunities are easily accessible to someone who has the ethical inclination and time for activism, and when that person feels peace is a compelling issue, the step into action is likely.

Persisters had extensive opportunities for peace action at the moment when they were ready to become involved. However, shifters and dropouts had the same opportunities when they joined the movement and they continue to have them, since all three groups are living in a metropolitan area where many peace organizations are active and seeking new members. But whether an activist seizes an opportunity depends on the perceived gravity of the situation. For example, the end of the Cold War offered activists with weaker beliefs or under other pressures the option to leave the movement, and they took it. On the other hand, persisters, because they felt a strong sense of personal responsibility and believed that peace action was still pressing, were more inclined to create their own opportunities at the end of a crisis by starting new groups or projects. Therefore, having a strong sense of personal responsibility and believing that peace action is urgent seem to bear directly on the continuation of commitment, while opportunity appears somewhat less significant by comparison.

Taking Action

Going to a rally, attending a peace group meeting, handing out literature are individual steps toward deeper involvement. Many commitments start in this way. Small steps are taken, which eventually lead to greater investments and sacrifices. Taking action, however small, can be a turning point, because it is action. By becoming active, a person establishes contact with other activists, their organizations and communities. This was how most of our activists became engaged in the work.

Peace commitments begin because people decide to act rather than merely contemplating action. They are available, the opportunity presents itself, the moment is right and they do it; they decide to approach the peace community and become involved. This step draws new activists into a deeper relationship with the issues of peace and nonviolence.

Joining a peace group can dramatically change the daily pattern of life as one shifts priorities and makes time for activism. It can also be a moral turning point caused by the pressing issues of historical circumstance. Wars and social movements set up a moral dilemma. Do nothing and play it safe or do something to stop the killing and social injustice, take a risk, and make a difference. As the issues of war and violence polarize people, there are mounting social pressures to resolve the dilemma by taking a stand and becoming involved in social activism. These pressures cause people to look carefully at themselves and where they stand ethically on the issues. If the decision of those who become activists is based on a greater awareness of their need or desire to live on "higher moral ground," the moral shift may become the basis of long-term peace activism.

In the accounts of the participants in our study, those social pressures were mentioned, as they were forced to look carefully at violence and social injustice, to struggle with the moral issues, then to become involved in social protest at the risk of public ridicule and physical harm. When a crisis forces such a decision, people may experience their step into activism as a transformation in their lives. This is a dramatic shift, not simply because they have joined a peace group, but because they have entered a new and more ethically grounded way of life.

A last minute decision to participate in a peace demonstration may lead an individual to become an activist if the moral question has been raised and if availability for activism is high. Once a person assumes an activist identity, opportunities for action may also be cultivated in the broader realm of national or global politics (through macromobilization) or in local communities (through micromobilization).

Commitment and Bonding

While national and global events and policies may be a major stimulant of activism, it is in the local settings, where most actions are planned and carried out, that peace commitments form and live. Those commitments arise through a process of bonding as the activist develops a feeling of loyalty to a peace group and to the movement as a whole.

The strength of a commitment can best be determined by observing how consistently a person pursues a particular course of action. Asking people how committed they are is a less reliable measure of their commitment than watching how they actually spend their time. We could not observe the everyday activity of our study participants, but their commitment could be roughly determined by how strongly they were bonded to their peace organizations and how those ties reinforced their commitments. We assessed the strength of these connections by asking them how much they agreed with something ("How much do you agree with the ethical principles of your peace group?"), how much they approved of it ("How do you feel about the job your peace group leaders are doing?"), or how emotionally attached to it they were ("How much does the peace community mean to you?").

Bonding to the Peace Group's Principles. How much activists value the principles of the peace group they join will influence the strength of their commitment. The more closely aligned a person's beliefs are with those principles, the greater the likelihood of bonding at the ideological level. There was a strong correspondence between our respondents' beliefs and their organization's principles, especially regarding the use of consensus decision-making, the emphasis on nonviolence, the linking of peace with social justice, and the strong undercurrent of environmental concerns. This ideological compatibility helped connect these activists to the broader peace movement, encouraged their participation, and strengthened their commitment.

They were attracted to peace communities which reflected and supported beliefs they already held. The contrary idea that people's beliefs are radically changed by joining a protest movement (the blind conversion hypothesis) is rooted in theories emphasizing the irrationality of social activists, which the growing evidence about participation in social movements does not support. The accounts of our respondents suggest that even the selection of a movement organization to join is, in large part, guided by conscious, rational decision-making. Persisters, shifters, and dropouts were all initially attracted to a peace organization because its espoused beliefs strongly reflected their own. Shifters and dropouts differed from persisters around the belief that peace action had become less important or because they felt their peace groups were not living up to peace movement principles. Thus, compatibility of beliefs affected the continuity of commitment for some.

Bonding to the Organization. The way people evaluate the performance of their peace organization is an important indicator of how attached to it they feel. Activists who bond to the organization are likely to express support for its goals and to show appreciation for its ways of working and handling internal conflict and external crises. The way a peace organization functions bears directly on its ability to preserve the commitments of its members. Participants must feel good about their organization: For the opportunities it provides for creativity, for the support it gives to individual efforts, for the positive working atmosphere it creates, and for the effectiveness of its operating style and democratic structures and procedures.

As a group, persisters reported positive feelings about how their peace groups were organized and run, despite some frustration with the length of time required to make decisions by consensus. In contrast, shifters and dropouts reported more conflicts with their organizations over policy or, if the organization was run in an autocratic way, over structure.

Bonding to Leaders. Expressions of appreciation and support for a peace organization's leaders indicate the presence of a bond to leadership. This attachment is likely to strengthen a member's commitment. Our respondents generally, but especially our persisters, felt that the leaders of their groups were performing well. Some of those leaders were even regarded as model peace activists. Yet, of the four types of bonding examined, personal attachment to leaders appeared to be the least important because of the peace movement's collective leadership ethic. With its emphasis on equality, participatory democracy, and shared responsibility, the movement places less importance on individual leaders and, in fact, there is a pronounced concern that such leaders not be elevated.

Consequently, bonding to leaders seemed less crucial in determining the commitment of these activists than other factors. More influential was their perception of how democratically and effectively their organizations operated, and how they felt about the people with whom they worked. Yet, most judged the leaders of their organizations to be good and effective people, so there was some loyalty to leaders as well.

There is a good chance that, had they felt differently, they would not have remained committed to their groups. We saw this in Monica's case when she left her group because of the arbitrary and dominating behavior of its leader. Thus, while bonding to leadership does not emerge as a major determinant of commitment continuity, it is still important in the sense that an ineffective leader may cause a member's commitment to weaken or collapse.

Bonding to the Peace Community. Positive feelings toward co-workers and close friendships with them indicate the presence of bonding to the peace community. If such relationships exist, a member's commitment will be strengthened and thus be more likely to survive. Of the connections we have discussed, the tie to community may be the most important, because human relationships mean so much to these people. Close relationships with others, mutual respect, and a common set of experiences draw them together into a community of caring and hope. These friendships can compensate for weaker links to other sectors of a movement, such as the organization or its leadership.

These activists developed close ties with their co-workers and acquired an appreciation for community, partly from the support and companionship they found there. But that community also represented a practical experiment in creating nonviolent social relations. For many persisters, the community of peacemakers was a refuge from mainstream society, where their values were appreciated and could be lived. There was a feeling of being at home there.

The nature of their attachments to the peace community varied among the shifters and dropouts. Some were solidly linked, others only loosely associated. While it seems clear that deep involvement in a peace community will encourage the preservation of commitment, it does not guarantee it. Even a commitment which is grounded in close ties to a peace community can be eroded by changes in a person's life circumstances. However, for someone who is well integrated into the peace community, those circumstances would have to be extreme; whereas, for someone with weaker community connections, less significant changes could have a major impact.

Since no bond by itself is likely to preserve a commitment, an activist's entire bonding pattern should be examined. We would want to know how many bonds exist: Is there attachment to the peace group's principles, to its organizational structure, to its leaders, and to the community? Also, what are the various strengths of each connection? For most of our persisters, all four of these bonds were present and, while their strength varied, they were solid enough to support a commitment over time. It should be noted that each person's commitment is a unique arrangement of these bonds and their relative strengths. For example, David did not have a strong relationship to the community, yet his commitment continued, which demonstrated that close attachment to a community is not absolutely necessary. His strong attachment to the principles of the movement and to the organization and its goals compensated for weak community ties.

Although space constraints prevent us from showing the full variation of commitment patterns among our respondents, we acknowledge the differences in order to emphasize that our theory of sustained commitment is a generalization which applies to them as a whole and not necessarily to specific cases. In reality, each person has a unique pattern of commitment.

Sharing the Peace Vision

Commonly held beliefs can be a powerful source of support for the survival of peace commitments. Persisters shared a vision of a peaceful world, agreed that eliminating war, violence, and social injustice was the way to realize that vision, and adopted peace activism as a life-long commitment. This vision was part of a shared reality continually reinforced within and outside their organizations through frequent communications with one another. This shared perception of a preferred future, its goals, and the means to achieve them integrated people into the community and provided them with a common world view. It also defined the problems to be solved, established a course of action, offered a rationale for continuing movement work, and produced a common discourse to give meaning and coherence to that work.

While the social reality shared by persisters may be similar to the perceptions of those who, like our shifters and dropouts, stayed active only for a while, it differed in an important respect. Persisters saw themselves as a small but dedicated group distinct from the thousands who dropped out of activism after a short time or who entered the movement at intervals in response to major crises. In short, persisters know they are persisters. They know they will keep at it, even while others come and go. The social reality they create requires them to witness for peace continuously by diligently educating the public about peace issues, organizing actions, and treating others according to the ethical principles of nonviolence. Sharing a perception of their unique persister role keeps them committed over the long term and creates a cohesiveness among them. This "staying power," combined with their vision of a peaceful world emerging sometime in the future, gives them the tenacity and confidence to continue their movement work.

Managing Commitment

Once an activist commitment forms, it must be managed if it is to endure. Activists must be creative in shaping the circumstances of their lives for long-term peace work. This might require changing their friendship patterns so they feel supported in their work and developing ways of responding to criticism so they are not immobilized by it. They must also balance and modify their larger array of life responsibilities to reinforce their peace careers as well as create burnout strategies to get through the hard times.

Managing Support for Peace Action. A peace commitment needs wholehearted backing from those with close personal ties to the activist. Persisters were encouraged by non-movement husbands, wives, children, parents and friends. Often those people made significant sacrifices of time and money so activist work could continue. In addition, strong and widespread encouragement came from other movement members. Those sources of internal and external support encouraged them to keep with the work, helped them deal with discouragement, and provided time and other resources so peace action could be pursued on a regular basis. If social support of this kind does not exist at the outset of an activist's career, it must be created.

Developing a peace commitment can produce dramatic changes in friendship, as ties weaken to friends who are lukewarm or resistant to peace action and more time is spent with fellow activists. As close personal friendships develop with other activists, a sense of community emerges which affirms the value of the work, while it provides sharing, caring, opportunities for cooperative action, and encouragement to keep the commitment going.

Persisters were especially sensitive to this need for enthusiastic support for their peace work and they created social lives where they received it. However, shifters and dropouts were also widely supported from inside and outside the movement, so this factor seems largely unimportant in explaining the differences of commitment between the three groups.

Managing Criticism. Peace activists cannot escape criticism from members of their extended family, acquaintances, or others in the wider community whose ideological leanings differ from their own. Our activists commonly used three responses to such criticisms: They discounted them, knowing they were based on irreconcilable differences of belief; they insulated themselves by eliminating or reducing their contact with the critics; and they employed humor to remove the sting from harsh words.

These methods worked in part because activists were generally supported by people who played more significant roles in their lives, such as family members and close friends. Criticism from more significant others was almost completely absent from the accounts of these activists. Had it existed, we would have expected it to either reduce the strength of their commitments or lead to the disruption of those relationships.

Managing Competing Responsibilities. An activist's commitment is set within a larger constellation of obligations to family, job, and friends. Persisters were less likely than shifters and dropouts to have responsibilities which competed with their activism. We did not anticipate how creative persisters would be in managing movement and non-movement demands. Many chose a materially simple life style so employment pressures did not interfere with their movement work. For example, some took or created jobs with flexible time schedules so they could more easily integrate peace action into their lives. Others took low-paying jobs in their peace groups which gave them especially valued opportunities for earning a living from peace action.

Our observation of the capacity peace persisters develop for organizing their lives around their activism is supported by Smith and Nepstad in their study of recruitment to high-risk activism.[2] They found the ability of activists to balance family and professional responsibilities in a career life situation to be an influential determinant of following through on their intention to participate in high-risk actions. Activist persistence, according to their study and ours, depended more on the skill of activists to organize multiple life responsibilities, than being free of such demands, as had been suggested by previous research.

Such creative management of responsibilities among our activists was possible in part because their immediate family and friends were willing to "take up the slack" so movement work could receive fuller attention. Thus, commitment is not merely an act of individual will: It also has a deeply social character. Others in an activist's life offer help and make sacrifices so the movement work can be done. Husbands, wives, children, and friends may all share the burden, such as assuming responsibilities the peace activist must neglect at home or work. At the very least, supporters must be willing to tolerate being neglected as the activist attends meetings, plans and carries out demonstrations, then retreats into solitude for recovery.

Persisters managed the competing demands on their time in a climate where others offered support, so their peace commitments survived. For shifters, it was not insurmountable problems with their responsibilities which led them to leave peace activism. Some simply changed their minds about the necessity for peace action, while others were dissatisfied with their peace groups. Dropouts were more inclined to leave the movement because of cross-pressures caused by career changes, marital and family matters, or financial need. Such problems can take on crisis proportions if a person has reached burnout and is looking for a way out of the movement.

Managing Burnout. To persevere as an activist, one must deal with burnout. Persisters and shifters, more than dropouts, were able to avoid it: They balanced action with reflection, diversified their activities, used creative outlets to relieve tension, withdrew into solitude or nature to regain their energy, found kindred spirits for mutual support, and developed long-term views of change in order to maintain their motivation.

Consciously developed and implemented, a burnout prevention plan can reduce the chances of a commitment collapse. The lives of our persisters revealed that balance is a key element in avoiding burnout. They refrained from working to the point of exhaustion, cared for personal needs as well as movement demands, and took time to play and create. Such efforts balanced the stresses and disappointments of peace work with spirit-renewing activities. Through this balancing act, burnout was avoided and an activist's commitment was sustained.

The Rewards of Peace Activism

Moral conviction and the pressing nature of a problem can keep peace activists going, even in the face of serious setbacks. Yet, there must be some rewards for persistence; at the very least, a perception that their action has made a difference. Thus, it is not surprising that, when a small victory is won, commitment seems to strengthen and motivation to rise. These modest successes are among the rewards of social activism.

While successes are important for keeping activists involved, they do find other rewards: The gratification of living in harmony with their values and becoming a more nonviolent person; the appreciation of other members and supporters of the movement; observing other activists living the ethics of nonviolence with one another and with opponents in the community; watching consensus decision-making resolve conflict and preserve a feeling of community; learning how to communicate and organize; and noticing that life is more meaningful for them as peace activists.

These less tangible rewards seemed to satisfy most persisters, guided as they were by a broader view of change: Of not just contributing to the creation of a more just and peaceful world, but of becoming more peaceful and effective people, capable of living an integrated life according to the principles of nonviolence. Seen in this light, long-term activists may initially join social movements in order to change society or solve global problems but, as a consequence of their participation, they may also change themselves and, through that change, create the possibility for a new kind of community.

COMMITMENT STRENGTH AND FLUCTUATION

Change is inherent in life. Social processes continually fluctuate. This is as true for a person's relationship to a peace group as it is for the strength of one's commitment to the larger movement. This waxing and waning of commitment is seen in our activists' discussion of the forces increasing and decreasing their commitment, and of burnout and recovery. So, commitment weakens or becomes stronger as conditions outside and within the activist change. Some of these forces can be managed; others cannot. For persisters, commitment varied within a fairly narrow range. Many factors influenced its strength. It increased to the extent that activists:

❖ Continued to hold beliefs which were in harmony with peace and social justice goals and means;
❖ planned their lives so they had time for peace action;
❖ continued to feel personally responsible for creating peace and social justice;
❖ pursued and created opportunities for peace action at the international, national, and local levels;
❖ continued to believe that peace action was urgent;
❖ remained bonded to peace movement principles, and to their peace organizations, leaders, and peace communities;
❖ continued to receive support for their peace commitments from outside and inside the movement;
❖ effectively managed their private and movement responsibilities and the competing demands on their time and energy;
❖ successfully and continually integrated peace action into their everyday lives as part of a well-established ethical/activist identity;
❖ developed and implemented a strategy for burnout control;

❖ continued to feel that the peace movement as a whole and their peace organizations were getting results;

❖ continued to benefit from their activism in the form of new skills and personal growth;

❖ maintained their long-term view of change, which made them more patient with the slow rate of progress, knowing they might not see the full fruits of their labor; and

❖ remained faithful to a common vision of a more just and peaceful future toward which human societies would gradually move.

These commitment-sustaining conditions emerged in the accounts of our activists as they discussed how they were able to remain committed for so many years.

ACTIVIST CAREERS

Many of these persisters developed "ethical careers." Some were entrepreneurs, like those observed by McCarthy and Zald in other movements.[3] Yet, while "entrepreneurial" in the sense that they created work for themselves, that work did not appear institutionalized and "mainstreamed" into conventional political channels. A few had modestly paid positions with peace organizations, but most persisted, not because they were making a living from peace activism, but out of a sense of mission. There is, of course, an institutionalized sector of the peace movement, run by professional peacemakers, but most of our persisters appeared to operate rather independently from it.

Persisters were similar in several respects to McAdam's Freedom Summer veterans.[4] Several had begun their activism in the civil rights movement. Many were working in education and the helping professions, with incomes lower than their relatively high educational achievement would lead one to predict. Support from their extended social networks appeared to be more important than the support they received from their movement organizations. Many moved from their initial step into activism as a moral stand to peace work as a vocation within a growing web of personal and organizational supports.

Career activism involved more profound life change for some of these activists than others. There were two broadly defined groups: Those who reshaped their lives around their activism and those who did movement work without a major life change.

These two paths illustrate Travisaro's distinction between conversion and alternation in social movement participation. Some participants' lives are transformed by total commitment to the cause. They become completely absorbed in the movement. Others are able to "commute" between the movement world and their conventional lives.[5]

CONCLUSION

Taken together, the many elements of our activists' stories are united in a model of sustained commitment, which appears in Figure 9.1. This model reveals the various influences which shape the beliefs of people during socialization so they become more attitudinally available for activism. It also identifies life pattern as an important determinant of their situational availability, giving them enough time and energy to act on their beliefs. Once available, their joining the movement is contingent on opportunity. When peace groups are nearby and plentiful, one who is fully available will be more likely to take the step into action. But opportunity must be continually cultivated by activists, either by responding to new projects others invent or by creating their own. The full exploitation of this personal opportunity structure is one of the important factors in the formation and maintenance of commitment. The others are: Creating an activist identity, which encompasses the ethic of helping others and personal responsibility; bonding to a peace group's ideology, organization, leadership, and community; managing the commitment once it forms, which includes continually arranging the pattern of everyday responsibilities to permit activism; maintaining the belief that peace action is urgent, which gives meaning to the work; continuing to be clear about the peace movement's vision and confident that change will eventually occur, which keeps motivation at a sufficiently high level; growing personally from movement work by developing new skills and a more nonviolent temperament; integrating peace action into everyday life; gaining support from significant others and responding constructively to criticism; and developing a strategy to avoid or handle burnout so commitment can be renewed. These factors operate within the macromobilization context where national and international events and policies help set the political agenda for local activists and within the micromobilization contexts where peace groups carry out their projects and tend to their community life.

153

Figure 9.1: A Model of Sustained Commitment

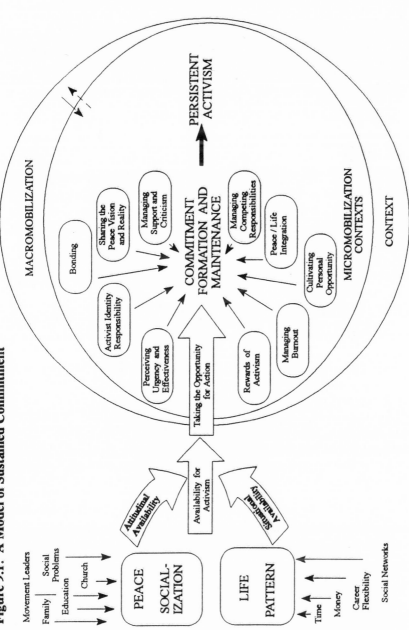

NOTES

1. J. Craig Jenkins, *The Politics of Insurgency.* (New York: Columbia University Press, 1985).

2. Christian Smith and Sharon Erickson Nepstad, "Biographical Stability and Relational and Organizational Ties in the U.S. Central America Peace Movement," unpublished paper, Department of Sociology, University of North Carolina, Chapel Hill, 1996.

3. John McCarthy and Mayer Zald, "Resource Mobilization and Social Movements: A Partial Theory," *op. cit.*, pp. 1212-1241.

4. Doug McAdam, "The Biographical Consequences of Activism," *op. cit.*, pp. 744-760.

5. See Richard Travisaro, "Alternation and Conversion as Qualitatively Different Transformations," in Gregory Stone and Harvey Farberman, eds., *Social Psychology Through Symbolic Interaction.* (New York: Wiley, 1981), pp. 237-248; and Doug McAdam, "The Biographical Consequences of Activism," *op. cit.*

10

COLLECTIVE
AND CREATIVE ACTION

Our theory of sustained commitment deepens and expands our knowledge of long-term participation in social movements, an area of research collective action theorists agree has been neglected. The stories of our activists suggest that all three sets of collective action theories we presented in the first chapter are partially correct.

IMPLICATIONS OF THIS STUDY FOR
COLLECTIVE ACTION THEORY

Social psychological theories assume that collective behavior arises largely from the characteristics of individual protestors, who, loosed from their normal social moorings, become susceptible to irrational impulses which arise as responses to social disorganization and isolation. Alongside of this "malintegration" hypothesis is the notion that idealistic beliefs can have powerful influences over the minds of people who are dissatisfied with social conditions.

This approach partially explains how our respondents were able to stay committed over the long term. Their commitments were heavily influenced by a transcendent world view, a generalized belief in the moral virtues and practical possibilities of living in a nonviolent world. Yet, the sufficiency of the malintegration thesis to explain protest behavior must be called into question. Our activists were led to the movement by the hope for a better world, not because they were socially isolated from mainstream society. They were not aberrant, unstable people. Rather, they were normal and stable individuals who were well integrated into society, but who, seeing the gap between the ideal and the real, became critical of the existing order and were determined to change it.

Rational choice theories explain social movement participation as a result of conscious decisions people make to reduce the costs and maximize the benefits of their effort. Thus, social activists are viewed as thoughtful, even calculating, decision-makers who control their social environment at least as much as it controls them. This study confirms, in part, this rational choice theory of social movement behavior.[1] Our career activists were deliberate, thoughtful architects of their own participation. The mobilization of their resources was rational and finely tuned. Their personal opportunity structures were carefully identified and fully exploited.

Rational choice was prominent in the decisions they made to participate and remain active. Selective incentives seemed to attract them to the movement and keep them there. These included paid positions in movement organizations and a sense of community and well-being. The collective goods of human survival and the promise of a better world were even stronger incentives. This mix of private and public rewards engaged them and kept them involved.

New Social Movements theory explains post-World War II movements as the response of largely middle class young people to new grievances which have developed from modernization processes and economic growth and the ever-increasing intrusion of powerful organizations into personal life. This approach emphasizes the development of unique cultural forms as a consequence of the day-to-day activities of social activists, who continually experiment with new ways of forming and organizing community.

The experiences of our persisters also partially validate this approach. Many of them "lived" the movement as an integral part of their daily lives. They created local projects rich in symbols which established their activist roles within distinct movement communities. Those communities were strengthened by a special discourse and mode of communicating, derived from their shared values and perceptions of social reality. Their activism was a response to what were perceived as new and immense threats from superstates and megacorporations, species-extinction possibilities and policies that denied fundamental human rights.

The demographic character of our activist group leads to some interesting speculation, since the majority were in their forties and fifties. Does this age composition suggest that contemporary persistent activists are uniquely a product of post-World War II social movements? New Social Movements theorists offer the view that post-war societal reconstruction was largely responsible for the decades of protest that followed it. If so, perhaps our persisters represent no more than a momentary blip on the screen of history. They may, nevertheless, be reproducing themselves by cultivating peace-oriented beliefs and practices in their children and proteges, in the same way they were influenced by other activists when they first began their peace careers. If not, will this cohort of persisters disappear as the post-World War II cycle of protest recedes further into the past? Still, these long-term persisters may stimulate the growth of new social movements as other survivors of declining movements have done.[2] Might they be the vanguard of a "footloose cadre" of activists working to develop a global nonviolence movement?

There was some indication among our respondents of this larger movement perspective. We found them to be less tied to specific movement organizations and leaders than we expected, an unusual characteristic for movement workers. A paramount concern of theirs was the creation of nonviolent social relations within a world of more equitably distributed wealth and life chances. They joined movement organizations where they felt that goal could be pursued and moved out of those where it could not. They maneuvered freely between groups as issues shifted and their interests changed, or in response to a particular group's effectiveness and sense of community. As Hunt and Benford have suggested, an activist's identity can become part of a collective identity rooted in the larger movement rather than in a movement organization.[3]

Some of our activists paid little attention to movement boundaries, thinking and acting freely for women's rights, the environment, and peace as the need for action arose. Their commitment seemed more to nonviolent social change broadly defined than to the goals of specific peace movement organizations. Their common focus on nonviolence may suggest the growth of a community of "kindred spirits" of one mind about

the need for a transformation of social and international relations. Their mobility across organizations and sometimes movements raises an interesting question for collective action
theorists. Is a metamovement developing which transcends national boundaries, whose focus is the elimination of violence?

These activists work within a global network of organizations
dedicated to the elimination of violence, though the size of that
network is not yet clear. Such a cadre, committed to an ideology
of nonviolence, would be ready to shift its participation into
specific action groups according to need and opportunity. It
would use movement organizations as convenient vehicles for
actualizing an ethical commitment to nonviolence. If such a
metamovement is developing, perhaps it is loyalty to the principles of nonviolence, more than to movement organizations,
which will sustain the commitment of its activists.[4] The unusual
character of such a movement would call for a new line of inquiry
in collective action research.

Our study of sustained activist commitment is a departure
from the main thrust of recent collective action research. There,
the focus has been on the life path of particular movements, and
especially their mobilization and institutionalization phases.
During those phases, large numbers of people are recruited for
relatively short periods, a few movement organizations take root
in institutional politics, and the rest of the movement dies. While
a movement's institutionalizing sector does, to a degree, keep its
goals alive as it declines, the movement's cutting edge is progres-
sively dulled by "business-as-usual."

Our findings suggest that an uninstitutionalized counterpart
within social movements has been developing over two decades,
in the form of life-long activists who continue to maintain the
cutting edge of protest. These persisters in communities
throughout the society, very active but not very visible to researchers, represent a continuing potential for movement maintenance and renaissance. They are a creative force counteracting
the inclination of national movement leaders to dull the edge of
protest in the interest of organizational self-preservation. With
their roots in local soil, their creative management of personal
resources, and their deep ideological conviction, persistent activists may be altering the structure and dynamics of social
protest quite unnoticed by mainstream research.

Our study thus suggests two new directions social movement research might take to understand more fully the changes movements undergo: Exploring the development of a protest infrastructure which counters the processes of decline and institutionalization that lead to the death of movements, and investigating the roles activist creativity and inventiveness play in determining movement vitality and longevity. We think the issue of activist innovation holds special promise for expanding our understanding of how activist commitment is managed and how social movements evolve and survive.

CREATIVE ACTION

Extending resource mobilization theory, we suggest that persistent activists are not only rational in how they choose a course of action, but they are also creative in identifying, mobilizing and combining their resources to pursue it. Their creativity appears in the day-to-day decisions they make in fashioning their lives, preventing burnout, designing and implementing projects, and even crafting their performance in court. Knowledge of this widespread creativity among activists is essential for understanding how the commitments of social activists develop and survive. We urge collective action researchers to turn more attention to what we will call "creative action," a neglected component of resource mobilization.

Creativity is connected to rationality, but it also has its own unique features: It is the process of exploring beyond conventional ways of thinking, behaving, and organizing. It draws on imagination and thrives on novelty and risk-taking. The term "innovation" best describes creativity, a process where people deal with changing conditions, develop new opportunities, and invent novel programs.

"Creative action theory" might address the question of how activist creativity affects the belief system of a movement, the character of its organization, its strategies of action, and how it mobilizes resources. It could also consider how movements in turn influence activist creativity. How is that creativity confined or encouraged by the movement's ideology, the character of its organizational structure, its decision-making process, and its style of leadership? It may be that some social movements encourage creativity on the part of their members, while others discourage it. Comparative studies of movements and their goals, structure, leadership, constituencies, ideologies and other potentially relevant factors bearing on creativity could give us valuable insights into movement effectiveness and permanence.

Social movements develop because their participants have insufficient power to make the changes they want by normal political means. This power disadvantage calls on the human spirit for innovation. The weaker challenger must be more creative to counterbalance the material resources of the strong and established; therefore creativity will be a normal and fundamental feature of social movements. Investigating creative action more fully, we may discover that creativity plays a major role in maintaining activist commitments, the power leverage of movements, and the viability of their organizations. While this issue may have been touched upon in studies of movement entrepreneurship, we believe that developing theories of creative action will raise interesting questions and stimulate new and valuable lines of collective action research.

NOTES

1. See William Gamson and Bruce Fireman, "Utilitarian Logic in the Resource Mobilization Perspective," in Mayer Zald and John McCarthy, eds., *The Dynamics of Social Movements.* (Cambridge, MA: Winthrop Publishers, 1979), pp. 8-45.

2. How this occurred in the post-war women's movement is described in Leila Rupp and Verta Taylor, *Survival in the Doldrums: The American Women's Rights Movement, 1945-60.* (New York: Oxford University Press, 1987).

3. Scott Hunt and Robert Benford, "Constructing Personal and Collective Identities: Identity Work in the Peace and Justice Movement, 1982-1991." A paper presented to the Society for the Study of Symbolic Interaction, Pittsburgh, 1992, p. 11.

4. For an expansion of this idea of nonviolence as a social movement, see Paul Wehr, "Commentary: Toward a History of Nonviolence," *Peace and Change,* 20 (1995), pp. 82-93.

11

EPILOGUE

We close by giving these activists their own voice, as they contemplated the question: "If you were advising leaders of the peace movement about how to sustain the commitment of its members, what would you recommend?" The breadth of ideas they offered was striking, for they know from personal experience what activists need in order to stay committed over the long term. Drawn together, their ideas can be arranged in the form of a letter to movement leaders.

Friends:

It is time to tell you what I need to stay involved in peace work. As you well know, this is not easy work. The world seems to be falling apart around us and our efforts to build peace haven't borne much fruit. It can be hard and disappointing work, and there are things you personally can do to help me. Things like pulling me aside and giving me encouragement. Just telling me you appreciate my effort and that I need to keep it up, that it's important work, that I shouldn't even think about giving it up.

Invite me to help build our peace organization or a program within it because when I'm involved, deeply involved, I feel like the peace movement is mine, is part of me, and I'm a part of it. Get me involved at that level and I'll stay active and motivated.

There are times when I wonder about the value of what I'm doing. Help me to see how my contribution matters and show me how our peace group and the movement as a whole is making progress, so that I can see something coming from my efforts and those of others.

Please talk about the conception of peace that is guiding this whole thing. I need to be reminded of that vision, because sometimes I get lost in the details and forget the larger picture. You can help to remind me of the world we're trying to create and of the values of love and community that are the foundation of our work. Keep reminding me about that. You see, I need to remember why peace work is important and that things can be made better, if only by a little. I need to know that, together, we can make some difference.

If you want to keep me motivated, give me something concrete to do in my community. I want to be involved in action that puts me in direct contact with people, around an issue that really touches me. The work in the wider world is important, but I also need something close by so I can be in contact with people who need my help. I need to talk to them, be with them, work with them. Such work puts me in situations where our peace and social justice vision really lives, where I can see some results.

I need people. That's why we must all pay more attention to building relationships, cultivating community. This has to be a conscious effort, not left to chance. We need to talk about it, work on it as we would on a peace action. We can only build what we really care about, so let's care more about community. When I feel I'm making this journey in community with other activists, I'm convinced that I could do this work forever. And when there are opportunities for working closely in intimate groups, small communities, I feel even more connected, because close friendships form, some that will last for a lifetime. Those friendships keep my commitment going.

Those small communities are important and we need to consciously develop them with each person who shows up for this work. And, even though we strive to live by the principles of equality and consensus, there are times when elitism still appears. Let's keep reminding one another how that is the past and not the future and discuss it, then change it. And, perhaps most importantly, we need to work hard to make our communities look like those of the future, with more diversity of color and culture. Let's begin to see this as a key part of our peace and justice work. At the moment, it's not something we feel compelled to do. It remains in the background. Let's put it up front and really work on it.

As leaders of the peace community, you and your work are appreciated, but sometimes you get lost in your tasks and forget about the rest of us, about how we just need to be with you and have a laugh together. Sometimes it seems like we're in such a hurry we forget to interact on a deeper human level. We forget the values we're working for. So, both of us trying to balance movement work with sharing could really make a difference.

As you try to connect with me as a person, know that I'm not simply a work machine, but have feelings with which you must help me. Give me opportunities for expressing my feelings and needs through peace work. Help me work with my emotions before I participate in an action and prepare me for other emotional responses that I can't even anticipate.

Teach me to live peace. Help me to learn how to be forthright in speaking the truth, as I understand it, not to be afraid. Help me to develop and demonstrate my love for humanity and encourage me to be open with others. Help me to bring a broader perspective to this work, to sustain my commitment. Help me learn to enjoy life, even in the face of so much misery in the world. Help me to lighten up and not be so serious all the time. Try to encourage my sense of humor. I do have one. I can be really funny at times, though this work can push humor into the background. Help me to laugh, even in the face of my disappointment.

Help me learn how to be a nonviolent and peaceful person, because I know that, if I haven't made peace within myself, I will have a hard time creating it in the world. Help all of us talk about inner peace and our own development, not just our obligation to the world. We can forget that the inner and outer worlds are really one. And to teach us, you, too, must try to live this peaceful inner life. I'm not asking that you be an example, only that you be in the struggle with me and that we help each other to truly live peace.

You see, if we can do this inner work and find that peace within ourselves, perhaps we could be more effective. Look at all the conflict within our group and the marathon meetings, where people just go on and on, driven by their own issues and forgetting the larger purpose. Couldn't we make better decisions if we actually talked about why we get so carried away and how we can change that? I would certainly feel more like coming to meetings if we were more effective there. Sometimes I really get discouraged by our in-fighting and ego turfing. Couldn't we work as hard on changing ourselves as we do on changing the world?

Even though I've been involved in peace and justice work for a long time, you must see my commitment as vulnerable, not unshakable. Look for my weariness and do something to help me avoid burnout. Don't keep calling on me for new assignments, even before my current work is completed. That overwhelms me. Instead, recruit new people for new projects. Don't take me for granted just because I've been at this a long time.

Too often, the movement doesn't grow because we rely on a small group of people who do all the work. We forget to invite others in, to make recruitment of new members a priority. We assume people will show up when there's a crisis, then hopefully stay. Perhaps there are other ways to continuously bring new people into our projects, even inviting them to join and start projects of their own.

Another way you could help me sustain my commitment is to create support groups within our organization so I have people to turn to when I'm down. If we consciously developed burnout prevention groups, everyone would have someone to rely on when things aren't going well.

Help me select realistic projects and goals so I don't get discouraged. Burnout is sometimes just caused by having an unrealistic project or an impossible goal. Help me find a project where I can feel effective and that will sustain my spirit and energy. And, let's not push one another to exhaustion. That destroys the balance I mentioned earlier.

Finally, I guess I need to be reminded again and again of the vision of the changes we're trying to bring about. When I forget that vision, it's discouraging when I don't see something happening that I want to have happen. Please keep reminding me that I'm building the foundation for a future I may never see. I wish it were otherwise, but at least the reminder will keep me going.

You know, we're all so busy we don't talk much about these things. Perhaps we should.

In peace,

This letter includes many of the down-to-earth thoughts these activists shared about how to keep peace commitment going. Leaders must have many of the same concerns, for their work is demanding and sometimes lonely and discouraging. Whatever role an individual takes within the movement, career peace action is difficult because it calls for enormous expenditures of time and energy, but promises few tangible rewards. It is for this reason that persisters are extraordinary. In an affluent society where most people want material success in order to live the comfortable life, this small community of peace activists reminds us that there is another vision and another way to live.

FURTHER COMMENTS
ON THE LITERATURE

The reader may wish to explore certain questions our book has raised. This brief essay of relevant literature may be useful. (Full citations of the sources can be found in the Bibliography.)

A very useful and comprehensive treatment of contemporary social movement theory is to be found in *International Social Movement Research*, Volume 1 (1988), Volume 2 (1989), Volume 3 (1991), edited by Bert Klandermans, Hanspeter Kriesi, and Sidney Tarrow. Of particular value to the present study is Klandermans' "The Peace Movement and Social Movement Theory," which appears in Volume 3 of that series. Also of special importance in that volume is Sam Marullo's "The U.S. Peace Movements in the 1980s."

Social disorder is particularly well covered in general terms by James Rule in *Theories of Civil Violence*. Charles Tilly's *From Mobilization to Revolution* examines protest historically as resource mobilization, while Ted Gurr, in *Why Men Rebel*, approaches disorder from a social disorganization perspective. Barrington Moore's *Injustice: The Social Bases of Obedience* focuses on the conditions under which the perception of unjust inequality stimulates protest. Theodore Lowi's *The Politics of Disorder* discusses how political systems manage institutional and extra-institutional challenges. Neil Smelser, in *A Theory of Collective Behavior*, and William Kornhauser, in *The Politics of Mass Society*, focus their explanations of collective behavior on the conditions which are either necessary for or contribute to the rise of social movements.

Since 1970, some researchers, reacting to what they saw as a preoccupation with macroanalytic themes, have looked more at the units of protest themselves. They have studied protest as a conscious process of movement-building, as well as how the larger society has responded to and interacted with social movement organizations and members. Representative of this work are William Gamson's *The Strategy of Social Protest*, John McCarthy and Mayer Zald's "Resource Mobilization and Social Movements: A Partial Theory," Doug McAdam's *Political Process and the Development of Black Insurgency, 1930-1970*, Peter Eisinger's "The Conditions of Protest Behavior in American Cities," and Sidney Tarrow's *Democracy and Disorder: Society and Politics in Italy, 1965-1975*. The last two works develop the concept of "political opportunity structure," as does Herbert Kitschelt in "Political Opportunity Structures and Political Protest."

Jurgen Habermas' *Legitimation Crisis* and Alain Touraine's *The Postindustrial Society* are seminal contributions to the formation of New Social Movements theory. Other works representing that perspective are Alberto Melucci's "The New Social Movements: A Theoretical Approach," Bert Klandermans and Dirk Oegema's "Potentials, Networks, Motivations and Barriers: Steps Toward Participation in Social Movements," and Claus Offe's "New Social Movements: Challenging the Boundaries of Institutional Politics."

The "free rider" critique, which discounts the influence of collective incentives in stimulating protest, is presented in Mancur Olson's provocative work, *The Logic of Collective Action: Public Goods and the Theory of Groups*. The free rider effect requires that movement leaders successfully mix collective and selective incentives to motivate sufficient numbers of people to participate. To illustrate, in the 1980s, the peace movement made the collective threat of nuclear war sufficiently personal to large numbers to create a selective incentive to work for nuclear disarmament. The conviction that nuclear weapons were evil and that nuclear powers could be persuaded to give them up approximates, perhaps, the "generalized belief" Smelser identifies as the source of movement mobilization in his *A Theory of Collective Behavior*.

The most comprehensive work on social movement organizations (SMOs) is John McCarthy and Mayer Zald's *The Trend of Social Movements in America: Professionalization and Resource Mobilization*. John Lofland in *Protest: Studies of Collective Behavior and Social Movements* and Gerlach and Hine in *People, Power, and Change: Movements of Social Transformation* emphasize the form and structure of SMOs. Others focus on how organizations mobilize participation through aligning their problem presentation and analysis (frames) with those of potential constituencies. David Snow, E. Burke Rochford, Jr., Steven Worden, and Robert Benford lay out this theoretical approach in "Frame Alignment Processes, Micromobilization and Movement Participation." Snow and Benford, in "Ideology, Frame Resonance and Participant Mobilization," explore the framing of an organization's belief system. Doug McAdam's "Micromobilization Contexts and Recruitment to Activism" examines the microprocesses, such as social networks, former movement experience and prior personal contacts with movement members, by which people are recruited into movements. Russell Curtis and Louis Zurcher inform us about the resource base that social movements find in institutional society in "Stable Resources of Protest Movements: The Multiorganizational Field."

The literature on sustained participation in social movements is rather thin. What happens to persons once they are in the movement and why they stay or leave has not been very well studied. Several works, however, suggest interesting directions that research on individual participation might take: On the issue of why people move in and out of protest movements, see Albert O. Hirschman's *Shifting Involvements: Private Interest and Public Action*; on activist role development, John Lofland's *Doomsday Cult*; on the influence of prior movement experience, Doug McAdam's *Freedom Summer: The Idealists Revisited*; on professionalization of participation, John McCarthy and Mayer Zald's *The Trend of Social Movements in America*, and Joyce Mushaben's "Reflections on the Institutionalization of Protest: The West German Peace Movement." On the related issue of caretaker organizations, see Aldon Morris' *Origins of the Civil Rights Movement*.

There are a number of biographical accounts of sustained individual participation in peace movements that provide insight into why peace activists remain committed. Among the more recent are Margaret Hope Bacon's *One Woman's Passion for Peace and Freedom: The Life of Mildred Scott Olmsted*, Anthony Bing's *Israeli Pacifist: The Life of Joseph Abileah*, Judith Porter Adams' *Peacework: Oral Histories of Women Peace Activists*, and Malcolm Saunders' *Quiet Dissenter*. Robert Holsworth's *Let Your Life Speak: A Study of Politics, Religion and Antinuclear Weapons*

Activism is a useful qualitative study of a number of activist careers in Richmond, Virginia. Our understanding of the biographical determinants of social movement participation has been substantially expanded by the work of Sharon Erickson Nepstad in her study "Nicaragua Libre: High-Risk Activism in the U.S.-Nicaragua Solidarity Movement," Ph.D. dissertation, University of Colorado at Boulder, 1996.

There are studies of the dynamics, organizations and members of contemporary peace movements that have been helpful to us: Charles Bolton's "Alienation and Action: A Study of Peace Group Members;" John Lofland's *Polite Protesters: The American Peace Movement of the 1980s*; Sam Marullo and Lofland's *Peace Action in the Eighties*; Marullo, Alexandra Chute, and Mary Anna Colwell's "Pacifist and Nonpacifist Groups in the U.S. Peace Movement of the 1980s;" Lofland's "The Soar and Slump of Polite Protest: Interactive Spirals and the Eighties Peace Surge;" and Thomas Rochon's *Mobilizing for Peace: The Antinuclear Movements in Western Europe*.

There is also literature we have consulted that examines the psychological and ethical determinants of commitment to collective action: David Adams' *Psychology for Peace Activists,* Edward Snyder's "Sustaining the Peacemaker: Spiritual Resources for the Long Haul," Rosabeth Kanter's *Commitment and Community*, Pamela Oliver's, "If You Don't Do It, Nobody Will," and George Rude's *Ideology and Popular Protest*.

Much good research has been done in recent decades on the use of nonviolent sanctions, or unarmed popular resistance to external invasion and internal repression. Gene Sharp's *The Politics of Nonviolent Action* is at the center of this work.

Finally, some have written about the difficulties of doing and presenting research simultaneously for academic and lay readers. The attendant risks are discussed in Barrie Thorne's "Political Activist as Participant Observer: Conflicts of Commitment in a Study of the Draft Resistance Movement in the 1960s," and in Randy Divinski, Amy Hubbard, J. Richard Kendrick, and Jane Noll's "Social Change as Applied Social Science: Obstacles to Integrating the Roles of Activist and Academic."

APPENDIX

1. What is your age?

2. What is the highest educational degree you've attained?

3. What is your occupation?

4. What is your approximate yearly income?

5. Do you make any income from your peace activism?

6. How long have you been a peace activist?

7. What were some of the influences which led you to become a peace activist?

8. What peace group(s) are you currently involved with?

   Probe: How long have you been involved?

   Probe: What has been the nature of your involvement?

9. What were some of the reasons you became attracted to the peace group you're currently involved with?

10. What impact would you say your peace group has had on the local, national, and/or international situation?

11. How satisfied are you with the achievement, up to this date, of your peace group?

12. How satisfied are you with the achievement of the peace movement as a whole?

13. How active in the peace movement are you at this time?

14. How would you characterize the strength of your commitment to the peace group you're involved in?

15. Under what circumstances has the strength of your commitment decreased?

> *Probe: What are the things which have happened to make you feel less committed to go on with your group's peace work?*

16. Under what circumstances has the strength of your commitment increased?

> *Probe: What are the things which have happened to make you feel more committed to go on with your group's peace work?*

17. What is it that motivates you to continue your peace work?

18. Are there any people, past or present, who, as examples of dedicated peace activists, have affected your own level of peace activism?

> *Probe: If yes, who are they and how have they affected your own motivation to be active?*

19. Roughly how much time are you currently putting into peace activism?

20. Do you at times consider dropping out of your peace group?

> *Probe: If so, for what reasons?*

> *Probe: If so, why do you continue?*

21. Do you at times consider dropping out of the peace movement as a whole?

> *Probe: If so, for what reasons?*

> *Probe: If so, why do you continue your commitment to the peace movement?*

22. Can you think of some reasons why someone might leave your peace group?

23. Do you know of any people who have left your peace group?

> *Probe: If so, what do you think were the reasons they left?*

24. Can you think of some reasons someone might want to drop out of the peace movement as a whole?

25. How would you describe the sense of personal responsibility you feel to work for peace?

> *Probe: If you do feel personally responsible, what led you to feel that way?*

26. Do you have close friends within your peace group?

> *Probe: If so, what effect do those friendships have on your commitment to the peace group's work?*

> *Probe: If so, how close would you say you are to those friends?*

27. What are the ethical principles you hold which seem connected to your peace work?

> *Probe: How similar are your ethical principles to those espoused by your peace group?*

> *Probe: Are there any differences between your ethical principles and your group's principles?*

> *Probe: If so, what are those differences?*

> *Probe: How serious are those differences?*

28. How strongly attached are you to your peace group's ethical principles? Explain.

29. How do you feel about your peace group's organization?

> *Probe: How do you feel about the way things are run?*

30. If you had to assess the job your peace group's leaders have done, what would you say?

31. Do you feel a sense of personal loyalty toward your peace group's leaders?

> *Probe: If so, how strong is that loyalty?*

32. Given the world situation today, how urgent would you say peace efforts are?

> *Probe: Has the feeling of urgency for peace action changed recently?*

> *Probe: If so, what changes or events have affected the feeling of urgency?*

33. Are there any individuals or groups outside of your peace group which support your peace work?

> *Probe: Who are the individuals? Which are the groups?*

> *Probe: What effect does that support have?*

34.   Are there any individuals or groups within your personal
      network that oppose your peace work?

      Probe: If so, who are the individuals? Which are the groups?

      Probe: What effect does that opposition have?

35.   Thinking of other commitments outside of your peace
      group, such as family and career, how much do these other
      commitments compete with your peace work?

      Probe: If there is competition, how do you handle it?

36.   Do you sometimes grow weary of being involved?

      Probe: What do you do when that happens?

37.   Thinking of other commitments outside of your peace
      group, such as family and career, how much do these other
      commitments reinforce your peace work?

      *Probe: How much, and in what ways, do they reinforce
      your commitment?*

38.   How is it that some people have remained strongly
      committed to peace work even during times of little
      progress and serious setbacks?

      *Probe: What makes them persist in their commitment in
      the face of such difficulties?*

      *Probe: What specific things do people do to maintain their
      commitments?*

39.   Would you say you have been one of these persisters?
      *(If it is clear they're a persister, say: "Since you are a persister,
      what factors have contributed to that persistence?" Then skip
      first probe.)*

      *Probe: If so, what are the factors which have contributed to
      your persistence as a peace activist?*

      *Probe: Are there specific things you have done, like
      developing certain coping strategies, which have
      allowed you to be committed over the long haul?
      If so, what?*

      Probe: If not, why?

40.   What kind of peace activist is likely to remain committed
      over the long haul?

41. If you were advising leaders of the peace movement about how to sustain the commitment of its members, what would you recommend?

42. What kind of impact has your peace activism had on your personal development?

    Probe: Has it changed your personality in any way?

43. Is there anything you'd like to add to explain how you've been able to persist as a peace activist over the long haul?

*This interview guide for persisters was modified in appropriate ways for the shifters and dropouts.

BIBLIOGRAPHY

Adams, David. *Psychology for Peace Activists: A New Psychology for the Generation Who Can Abolish War*. (New Haven, CT: The Advocate Press, 1989).

Adams, Judith Porter. *Peacework: Oral Histories of Women Peace Activists*. (Boston: Twayne Publishers, 1991).

Bacon, Margaret Hope. *One Woman's Passion for Peace and Freedom: The Life of Mildred Scott Olmsted*. (Syracuse, NY: Syracuse University Press, 1993).

Becker, Howard S. "Notes on the Concept of Commitment," *American Journal of Sociology*, 66 (1960), pp. 32-40.

Berger, Peter and Thomas Luckman. *The Social Construction of Reality*. (New York: Doubleday, 1966).

Bing, Anthony. *Israeli Pacifist: The Life of Joseph Abileah*. (Syracuse, NY: Syracuse University Press, 1990).

Bolton, Charles. "Alienation and Action: A Study of Peace Group Members," *American Journal of Sociology*, 78 (1972), pp. 537-561.

Carden, Maren. "The Proliferation of a Social Movement: Ideology and Individual Incentives in the Contemporary Feminist Movement," in Louis Kriesberg, ed., *Research in Social Movements, Conflicts and Change*, Vol. 1 (Greenwich, CT: JAI Press, 1978), pp. 179-196.

Curtis, Russell and Louis Zurcher, Jr. "Stable Resources of Protest Movements: The Multiorganizational Field," *Social Forces*, 52 (1973), pp. 53-60.

Divinski, Randy, Amy Hubbard, J. Richard Kendrick, and Jane Noll, "Social Change as Applied Social Science: Obstacles to Integrating the Roles of Activist and Academic," *Peace and Change*, 19 (1994), pp. 3-24.

Downton, James V., Jr. *Rebel Leadership: Commitment and Charisma in the Revolutionary Process*. (New York: The Free Press, 1973).

Downton, James V., Jr. *Sacred Journeys: The Conversion of Young Americans to Divine Light Mission*. (New York: Columbia University Press, 1979).

Downton, James V., Jr. "Spiritual Conversion and Commitment: The Case of Divine Light Mission," *Journal for the Scientific Study of Religion*, 19 (1980), pp. 381-396.

Downton, James V., Jr. and Paul E. Wehr. "Peace Movements: The Role of Commitment and Community in Sustaining Member Participation," in Metta Spencer, ed., *Research in Social Movements, Conflicts, and Change*, Vol. 13. (Greenwich, CT: JAI Press, 1991), pp. 113-134.

Eisinger, Peter. "The Conditions of Protest Behavior in American Cities," *American Political Science Review*, 67 (1973), pp. 11-28.

Gamson, William. *The Strategy of Social Protest*. (Homewood, IL: Dorsey, 1975).

Gamson, William and Bruce Fireman. "Utilitarian Logic in the Resource Mobilization Perspective," in Mayer Zald and John McCarthy, eds., *The Dynamics of Social Movements*. (Cambridge, MA: Winthrop, 1979), pp. 8-45.

Gamson, William. "Political Discourse and Collective Action," in Bert Klandermans, Hanspeter Kriesi and Sidney Tarrow, eds., *International Social Movement Research*, Vol. 1. (Greenwich, CT: JAI Press, 1988), pp. 219-244.

Gerlach, Luther and Virginia Hine. *People, Power and Change: Movements of Social Transformation*. (Indianapolis: Bobbs-Merrill, 1970).

Goffman, Erving. *Presentation of Self in Everyday Life*. (New York: Doubleday Anchor, 1959).

Gurr, Ted. *Why Men Rebel*. (Princeton, NJ: Princeton University Press, 1970).

Habermas, Jurgen. *Toward a Rational Society*. (Boston: Beacon Press, 1970).

Habermas, Jurgen. *Legitimation Crisis*. (Boston: Beacon Press, 1973).

Hannon, James. "Becoming a Peace Activist: A Life Course Perspective," in Sam Marullo and John Lofland, eds., *Peace Action in the Eighties*. (New Brunswick, NJ: Rutgers University Press, 1990), pp. 217-232.

Hirschman, Albert O. *Shifting Involvements: Private Interest and Public Action*. (Princeton, NJ: Princeton University Press, 1982).

Holsworth, Robert. *Let Your Life Speak: A Study of Politics, Religion and Antinuclear Weapons Activism*. (Madison, WI: University of Wisconsin Press, 1989).

Hopper, Joseph and Joyce McCarl Nielsen. "Recycling as Altruistic Behavior," *Environment and Behavior*, 23 (1991), pp. 195-220.

Hunt, Scott and Robert Benford. "Constructing Personal and Collective Identities: Identity Work in the Peace and Justice Movement, 1982-1991." A paper presented to the Society for the Study of Symbolic Interaction, Pittsburgh, 1992.

Jacobi, Jolande. *The Way of Individuation.* (New York: New American Library, 1967).

Jenkins, J. Craig. *The Politics of Insurgency.* (New York: Columbia University Press, 1985).

Jung, Carl G. Commentary in Richard Wilhelm's *Secret of the Golden Flower.* (New York: Harcourt, Brace and World, Inc., 1931).

Jung, Carl G. *Mysterium Coniunctionis,* Volume XX of his Collected Works. (Princeton, NJ: Princeton University Press, 1970).

Kanter, Rosabeth. *Commitment and Community: Communes and Utopian Sociological Perspective.* (Cambridge, MA: Harvard University Press, 1972).

Kendrick, J. Richard, Jr. "Meaning and Participation: Perspectives of Peace Movement Participants," in Metta Spencer, ed., *Research in Social Movements, Conflicts and Change,* Vol. 13. (Greenwich, CT: JAI Press, 1991), pp. 91-111.

Kitschelt, Herbert. "Political Opportunity Structures and Political Protest," *British Journal of Political Science,* 16 (1986), pp. 57-85.

Klandermans, Bert and Dirk Oegema. "Potentials, Networks, Motivations and Barriers: Steps Toward Participation in Social Movements," *American Sociological Review,* 52 (1987), pp. 519-531.

Klandermans, Bert. "The Formation and Mobilization of Consensus," in Bert Klandermans, Hanspeter Kriesi, and Sidney Tarrow, eds., *International Social Movement Research,* Vol. 1. (Greenwich, CT: JAI Press, 1988), pp. 173-196.

Klandermans, Bert. "The Peace Movement and Social Movement Theory," in Bert Klandermans, Hanspeter Kriesi, and Sidney Tarrow, eds., International Social Movement Research, Vol. 3. (Greenwich, CT: JAI Press, 1991), pp. 1-42.

Knudson-Ptacek, Carmen. "Self Conceptions of Peace Activists," in Sam Marullo and John Lofland, eds., *Peace Action in the Eighties.* (New Brunswick, NJ: Rutgers University Press, 1990), pp. 233-245.

Kornhauser, William. *The Politics of Mass Society.* (New York: The Free Press, 1959).

Kriesi, Hanspeter. "Local Mobilization for the People's Petition of the Dutch Peace Movement," in Bert Klandermans, Hanspeter Kriesi and Sidney Tarrow, eds., *International Social Movement Research,* Vol. 1. (Greenwich, CT: JAI Press, 1988), pp. 41-82.

Lichbach, Mark. "What Makes Rational Peasants Revolutionary?" *World Politics,* 46 (1994), pp. 382-417.

Lofland, John. *Doomsday Cult.* (Englewood Cliffs, NJ: Prentice-Hall, 1966).

Lofland, John. *Protest: Studies of Collective Behavior and Social Movements.* (New Brunswick, NJ: Transaction Books, 1985).

Lofland, John. *Polite Protesters: The American Peace Movement of the 1980s.* (Syracuse, NY: Syracuse University Press, 1991).

Lofland, John. "The Soar and Slump of Polite Protest: Interactive Spirals and the Eighties Peace Surge," *Peace and Change,* 17 (1992), pp. 34-59.

Lowi, Theodore. *The Politics of Disorder.* (New York: Basic Books, 1971).

Marullo, Sam and John Lofland, eds., *Peace Action in the Eighties.* (New Brunswick, NJ: Rutgers University Press, 1990).

Marullo, Sam. "The U.S. Peace Movements in the 1980s," in Bert Klandermans, Hanspeter Kriesi, and Sidney Tarrow, eds., *International Social Movement Research,* Vol. 3. (Greenwich, CT: JAI Press, 1991), pp. 227-230.

Marullo, Sam, Alexandra Chute, and Mary Anna Colwell, "Pacifist and Nonpacifist Groups in the U.S. Peace Movement of the 1980s," *Peace and Change,* 16 (1991), pp. 235-259.

Marwell, G. "Altruism and the Problem of Collective Action," in V. Derlega and J. Grzelak, eds., *Cooperation and Helping Behavior.* (New York: Academic Press, 1982), pp. 13-37.

McAdam, Doug. *Political Process and the Development of Black Insurgency, 1930-1970.* (Chicago: University of Chicago Press, 1982).

McAdam, Doug. "Recruitment to High-Risk Activism: The Case of Freedom Summer," *American Journal of Sociology,* 92 (1986), pp. 64-90.

McAdam, Doug. *Freedom Summer: The Idealists Revisited.* (New York: Oxford University Press, 1988).

McAdam, Doug, John McCarthy and Mayer Zald. "Social Movements," in Neil Smelser, ed., *Handbook of Sociology.* (Beverly Hills, CA: Sage Publications, 1988), pp. 695-737.

McAdam, Doug. "Micromobilization Contexts and Recruitment to Activism," in Bert Klandermans, Hanspeter Kriesi and Sidney Tarrow, eds., *International Social Movement Research,* Vol. 1. (Greenwich, CT: JAI Press, 1988), pp. 125-154.

McAdam, Doug. "The Biographical Consequences of Activism," *American Sociological Review,* 54 (1989), pp. 744-760.

McCarthy, John and Mayer Zald. *The Trend of Social Movements in America: Professionalization and Resource Mobilization.* (Morristown, NJ: General Learning Press, 1973).

McCarthy, John and Mayer Zald. "Resource Mobilization and Social Movements: A Partial Theory," *American Journal of Sociology,* 82 (1977), pp. 1212-1241.

Melucci, Alberto. "The New Social Movements: A Theoretical Approach," *Social Science Information,* 19 (1980), pp. 199-226.

Melucci, Alberto. "Getting Involved: Identity and Mobilization in Social Movements," in Bert Klandermans, Hanspeter Kriesi and Sidney Tarrow, eds., *International Social Movement Research*, Vol. 1. (Greenwich, CT: JAI Press, 1988), pp. 329-348.

Melucci, Alberto. "The Process of Collective Identity." A paper presented at the Workshop on Culture and Social Movements, University of California, San Diego (June, 1992).

Miller, Byron. "Political Empowerment, Local-central State Relations, and Geographically Shifting Political Opportunity Structures," *Political Geography*, 13 (1994), pp. 393-406.

Moore, Barrington. *Injustice: The Social Bases of Obedience.* (White Plains, NY: M.E. Sharpe/Pantheon, 1978).

Morris, Aldon. *Origins of the Civil Rights Movement.* (New York: The Free Press, 1984).

Mushaben, Joyce. "Reflections on the Institutionalization of Protest: The West German Peace Movement, *Alternatives*, IX (1984), pp. 519-539.

Nepstad, Sharon Erickson. "Nicaragua Libre: High-Risk Activism in the U.S.-Nicaragua Solidarity Movement," Ph.D. dissertation, University of Colorado at Boulder, 1996.

Oberschall, Anthony. *Social Conflict and Social Movements.* (Englewood Cliffs, NJ: Prentice-Hall, 1973).

Offe, Claus. "New Social Movements: Challenging the Boundaries of Institutional Politics," *Social Research*, 52 (1985), pp. 817-868.

Oliver, Pamela. "If You Don't Do It, Nobody Will: Active and Token Contributors to Local Collective Action," *American Sociological Review*, 49 (1984), pp. 601-610.

Olson, Mancur. *The Logic of Collective Action: Public Goods and the Theory of Groups.* (Cambridge, MA: Harvard University Press, 1965).

Patfoort, Pat. *Uprooting Violence: Building Nonviolence.* (Freeport, ME: Cobblesmith, 1995).

Piven, Frances Fox and Richard Cloward. "Normalizing Collective Protest," in Aldon Morris and Carol Mueller, eds., *Frontiers of Modern Social Movement Theory.* (New Haven, CT: Yale University Press, 1992), pp. 301-325.

Rochon, Thomas. *Mobilizing for Peace: The Antinuclear Movements in Western Europe.* (Princeton, NJ: Princeton University Press, 1988).

Rude, George. *Ideology and Popular Protest.* (New York: Pantheon, 1980).

Rule, James. *Theories of Civil Violence.* (Berkeley, CA: University of California Press, 1988).

Rupp, Leila and Verta Taylor. *Survival in the Doldrums: The American Women's Movement, 1945-60.* (New York: Oxford University Press, 1987).

Saunders, Malcolm. *Quiet Dissenter.* (Canberra: Peace Research Center, Australian National University, 1993).

Schwartz, S.H. "Words, Deeds and the Perception of Consequences on Responsibility in Action Situations," *Journal of Personality and Social Psychology,* 10 (1968), pp. 232-242.

Sharp, Gene. *The Politics of Nonviolent Action.* (Boston: Porter Sargent, 1973).

Smelser, Neil. *A Theory of Collective Behavior.* (New York: The Free Press, 1962).

Smith, Christian and Sharon Erickson Nepstad. "Biographical Stability and Relational and Organizational Ties in the U.S. Central America Peace Movement," unpublished paper, Department of Sociology, University of North Carolina, Chapel Hill, 1996.

Snow, David, Louis Zurcher, Jr. and Sheldon Ekland-Olson. "Social Networks and Social Movements: A Microstructural Approach to Differential Recruitment," *American Sociological Review,* 45 (1980), pp. 787-801.

Snow, David, E. Burke Rochford, Jr., Steven Worden, and Robert Benford. "Frame Alignment Processes, Micromobilization and Movement Participation," *American Sociological Review,* 51 (1986), pp. 464-481.

Snow, David and Robert Benford. "Ideology, Frame Resonance and Participant Mobilization," in Bert Klandermans, Hanspeter Kriesi, and Sidney Tarrow, eds., *International Social Movement Research,* Vol. 1. (Greenwich, CT: JAI Press, 1988), pp. 197-217.

Snyder, Edward. "Sustaining the Peacemaker: Spiritual Resources for the Long Haul," *Quaker Life.* (July-August, 1982).

Solo, Pam. *From Protest to Policy: Beyond the Freeze to Common Security.* (Cambridge, MA: Ballinger, 1988).

Suarez, Rick, Roger C. Mills, and Darlene Stewart. *Sanity, Insanity, and Common Sense.* (New York: Fawcett Columbine, 1987).

Tarrow, Sidney. *Democracy and Disorder: Society and Politics in Italy, 1965-1975.* (Oxford: Oxford University Press, 1988).

Tarrow, Sidney. "Struggle, Politics, and Reform: Collective Action, Social Movements, and Cycles of Protest," Western Societies Program Paper No. 21. (Ithica, NY: Cornell University Press, 1989).

Thorne, Barrie. "Political Activist as Participant Observer: Conflicts of Commitment in a Study of the Draft Resistance Movement in the 1960s," *Symbolic Interaction,* 2 (1979), pp. 73-88.

Tilly, Charles. *From Mobilization to Revolution.* (Reading, MA: Addison-Wesley, 1978).

Touraine, Alain. *The Postindustrial Society.* (New York: Random House, 1971).

Travisaro, Richard. "Alternation and Conversion as Qualitatively Different Transformations," in Gregory Stone and Harvey Farberman, eds., *Social Psychology Through Symbolic Interaction.* (New York: Wiley, 1981), pp. 237-248.

Wehr, Paul. *Conflict Regulation.* (Boulder, CO: Westview Press, 1979).

Wehr, Paul. "Nuclear Pacifism as Collective Action," *Journal of Peace Research,* 23 (1986), pp. 103-113.

Wehr, Paul. "Commentary: Toward a History of Nonviolence," *Peace and Change,* 20 (1995), pp. 82-93.

INDEX